Battle Colors Volume II

BATTLE COLORS
Insignia And Aircraft Markings Of The Eighth Air Force In World War II

Volume II / (VIII) Fighter Command

Robert A. Watkins

Schiffer Military History
Atglen, PA

This volume is respectively dedicated to all the fighter pilots,
bomber and ground crews of the US Eighth Air Force,
especially those who never made it home.

Book Design by Robert A. Watkins.

Copyright © 2006 by Robert A. Watkins.
Library of Congress Control Number: 2003116219

Printed in China.
ISBN: 0-7643-2535-3

We are interested in hearing from authors with book ideas on related topics.

Published by Schiffer Publishing Ltd.
4880 Lower Valley Road
Atglen, PA 19310
Phone: (610) 593-1777
FAX: (610) 593-2002
E-mail: Info@schifferbooks.com.
Visit our web site at: www.schifferbooks.com
Please write for a free catalog.
This book may be purchased from the publisher.
Please include $3.95 postage.
Try your bookstore first.

In Europe, Schiffer books are distributed by:
Bushwood Books
6 Marksbury Avenue
Kew Gardens
Surrey TW9 4JF, England
Phone: 44 (0) 20 8392-8585
FAX: 44 (0) 20 8392-9876
E-mail: Info@bushwoodbooks.co.uk.
Visit our website at: www.bushwoodbooks.co.uk
Free postage in the UK. Europe: air mail at cost.
Try your bookstore first.

Contents

This, the second volume in the Battle Colors series, concludes the focus on 8th Army Air Force insignia & markings. This in no way is meant to imply that the 'book is closed' on this matter, quite the contrary. After spending better than fifty years in an avocational pursuit of this subject, I am constantly amazed at the regularity with which new images and data relating to continue to surface. One would tend to feel that given this age of 'super information' in which we now live that just about anything and everything there is to know about the subject of World War II would by now be a matter of public record. This is simply not the case however. Much of this new material is uncovered by professional historians who spend untold hours pouring over dusty archives, personal correspondence and photographic images. To these individuals the rest of us enthusiasts are truly indebted. However a surprising source of new or obscure information comes from either the veterans themselves or, in more recent years, a relative or close friend. For me personally this latter group has proven to be an invaluable source of data regarding the US Army Air Corps in the early to mid Twentieth Century, especially concerning the squadron and group levels. Whether the information concerns an unauthorized insignia or a particular theater of operations aircraft markings, these private sources can often provide a fresh insight into matters long overlooked and nearly forgotten with the passage of time. In some cases the photos / documentation I receive may be completely new in nature, in others it may serve to clear up some issue previously in question. It is with these private sources in mind that I have included below my mailing address.

Robert A. Watkins
8462 Road 41
Mancos, CO 81328-8945
USA

It is my hope that any individual in possession of information relating to US Army Air insignia and / or aircraft markings will take the time to forward a copy of that information on to me. It makes no difference what time period is represented as I am constantly looking for material on this subject dating anywhere from between the years 1916 through 1947. All such materials received will not only be welcome but put to good use in future works in an ongoing effort to preserve the images of the US Army Air Corps.

USAAF Camouflage & Markings

Since the advent of aerial warfare early in the Twentieth Century it has been observed that one can determine how close any given country is to going to war simply by observing their military aircraft. While this might be an oversimplification, there is nevertheless considerable merit in such a statement. As war clouds began to gather, once shinny military aircraft began to display an assortment of camouflage paint schemes. Although this adage may not necessarily apply today as much as it did in past conflicts, the fact is that in times of peace there simply were few logical reasons for the application of paint to the exterior of a metal finished aircraft. In addition to the obvious investment of materials and man-hours necessary for applying the paint, there is a decrease in fuel efficiency due to the additional weight and increased coefficient of friction or 'drag'. Slower and less maneuverable are characteristics one would not normally assign to any combat aircraft. It is thus easy to see why painting an aircrafts fuselage and wing surface area was something to be avoided unless so mandated by extreme necessity. That necessity arose, and still does arise, in time of war when opposing forces possess similar offensive capabilities i.e. the ability of both belligerents to attack each other's airfields. It was under these very conditions that air forces around the world learned very early on that it was not advisable to present an attacking force with shinny stationary aircraft as targets. Unfortunately the most expedient, versatile method of diminishing the profile of an airframe is with paint. Even the most elaborate of camouflage paint jobs however was no sure guarantee against detection by an attacking aircraft. The photo above how an airframes contour outline can provide convienant aiming points for enemy pilots.

The position of the sun, cloud cover, angle of attack, all were factors that could aid or detract from the effectiveness of almost any attempt to obliterate the profile of a stationary aircraft. Many alternate methods of concealment from attacking forces were utilized to one extent or another during the course of World War II including camouflage netting, foliage canopies and dugout revetments. Effective concealment involved man-hours, materials and a significant reduction to a fighters combat readiness response time. Given the highly mobile nature of WWII, surface paint proved to be the only consistently viable solution to the problem of profile disruption for most belligerents during the majority of this conflict. The ever-increasing presence of USAAF combat aircraft over the skies of Great Britain and Western Europe brought about the need for an improved means of unit identification for both fighter and bombers alike. Eighth AAF aircraft soon displayed a typical two-color overall paint scheme, brightly colored (and

highly visible) nose and tail patterns. These obviously offset any concealment advantages obtained with camouflage paint. By the time these high profile unit identification patterns began appearing however, Allied air power had seriously hampered the Luftwaffes ability to mount significant offensive sorties against Allied air bases in England. This was a transitional period in the European air war and the Luftwaffe would soon find itself incapable of virtually any offensive efforts whatsoever. Even so the Allied air forces were not about to become complacent where the Luftwaffe was concerned. There was considerable discussion regarding the advisability of issuing of SHAEF Operation Memorandum Number 23 of 18Apr44/Distinctive Markings-Aircraft, better known to the world as D-Day or Invasion Stripes. Admittedly there was a definite need for an improved system of 'friendly Allied aircraft' identification marks during and immediately following the Normandy Invasion but a series of large alternating black & white stripes on fuselage, wings and empennage was hardly conducive to conceal ment from an enemy aerial attack. There was considerable speculation at the time that the Luftwaffe might mount a massive retaliatory raid against Allied air bases in East Anglia and these tactical recognition markings would provide German pilots, gunners and bombardiers with a prime aiming point. Fortunately for the Allied cause the once mighty Luftwaffe found itself incapable of such a reprisal raid and the concern proved to be a mute point, at least until British and American fighter units were later redeployed to the European Continent. Once on European soil the new Allied air bases came within range of the Luftwaffe home defence fighters. The controversial D-Day Invasion Stripes quickly disappeared from the redeployed Allied units for the reason previously stated.

As the war continued to progress in the Allies factor, the combat aircraft of the Eighth began to take on a new look. With the threat of potential Luftwaffe attacks on Allied airfields based in England virtually eliminated, Eighth USAAF fighters and bombers alike began to rapidly shed their existing camouflage paint schemes and were soon reaping the benefits inherent with a natural metal finished fuselage and wing surface areas. Some ground crews would soon go as far as polishing and even waxing the entire fuselage and wings of the fighters in their charge. This was in an effort to maximize airflow over and around the airframe surface areas. The intent was to provide the men flying these aircraft with a little extra advantage, an advantage that in combat will often prove to be the deciding factor separating victory from defeat.

Prior to the outbreak of World War I the French Army foresaw the need for both national as well as individual markings on their aircraft, and thus brought into existence the first regulated and uniform method of aircraft identification. A tricolor circular devise, or cockade, was chosen to officially represent the air arm of the French Army. Germany would follow suit soon after with the introduction a Maltese or 'iron cross' selected to represent their country. This would eventually evolve into the Balkankreuz used by German military forces, air and land during World War II, which of course included the swastika on most tail surfaces. Great Britain's Royal Flying Corps originally adopted the Cross of St. George for its aircraft but a later revised WW I emblem was based upon the French cockade. The United States would similarly adopt a circular configuration for its national insignia but this was to undergo numerous changes up until and throughout World War II. Although though somewhat outside the immediate scope of this particular work, World War II specifically, a brief history of all US Army aircraft insignia has been included herein:

Circa 1916: Introduced at the North Island Aviation School in California, the first markings utilized by the Army Signal Corps was the image in the foreground. The background image incorporating the white circle was a briefly used unauthorized variation. Neither design was ever officially adopted by the Army for use as a national emblem. There were no images displayed on either the fuselage or wing surfaces.

•**May 17th, 1917**•
First authorized insignia and tail markings for US military aircraft. The colors varied significantly and were loosely in compliance with those used in conjunction with the American flag. This combination was used briefly on US aircraft in Europe during World War I.

•**January 11th, 1918**•
This cokarde pattern replaced the 'star in circle' design on US aircraft operating with Allied forces in Western Europe. This insignia was located on the right and left wing surfaces both top and bottom.The background image was the first pattern tail marking which was later replaced by the overlapping image. All US military aircraft were directed to reinstate the original 1917 'star' insignia in May of 1919.

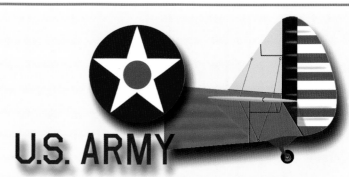

U.S. ARMY

The tail configuration was modified in 1927 to display a blue vertical stripe positioned at the rudderpost. This device was accompanied by a pattern of thirteen alternating red and white horizontal stripes trailing the blue stripe. The US Army letter designator, adopted in 1924, were applied to the under surface area of the ships wing (lower wing of biplanes). Both the tail marking and letter designator were dropped within six months of Pearl Harbor and neither devise was to ever again reappear on US Army aircraft. In 1940 the national insignia was directed to be applied to both sides of the fuselage for the first time. Additionally this same devise was ordered removed from the top right and lower left wings tips. This directive was intended to unbalance what had been perceived as a convenient aiming point, from both above and below, for enemy gunners.

•**May 28th, 1942**•
The red inner circle device was ordered discontinued due to problems in the Pacific Theater confusing the American emblem with the Japanese Hinomaru or 'Meatball' insignia used by that country.

•**October 9th, 1942**•
A two inch yellow outline was directed to be added to AAF aircraft serving in both Great Britain and North Africa (Nov.'42). The use of this devise was discontinued in both Theaters of Operation by April 1943.

An unofficial variation that appeared with regularity within the Eighth AAF structure was that of a grayed-out star contained within the national emblem. This again was an attempt to reduce a convenient aiming point for enemy gunners and pilots.

•**June 29th, 1943**•
In an ongoing attempt to provide US pilots with an improved recognition factor, the new 'Star-and-Bars' insignia was selected to replace the existing circular configuration. The red border was to be short lived and would ultimately be replaced with a blue outline. Another brief variation in the ETO was the addition of yellow inner 'bars'.

August 14th, 1943

The final USAAF National Insignia pattern which would remain unchanged throughout the remainder of World War II. The graphics below provide the specific orders as they relate to the modification of each US National Insignia presented.

| NO.24102-K | NO.24102-K AMMENDENTNO.3 | OPERATION MEMORANDUM NO.9 | UAAAF/AN-I-9A | UAAAF/AN-I-9B |

TYPE-1   **TYPE-2A**   **TYPE2B**   **TYPE-3A**   **TYPE-3B**

The many modifications to US aircraft insignia from December 1941 thru August 1943 were the result of a need to provide American aircrews with an extra margin of safety against friendly fire incidents. The dangers inherent with combat were bad enough without the additional risk of being shot down by your own people. In late 1942 thru early 1943 the Army/Navy Aeronautical board conducted a series of tests from air bases located in Florida. American aircraft, principally P-47s, were affixed with a wide range of insignia representing not only the US and its major allies, but the insignia of the Axis powers as well. In a series of fly-by runs at varying distances, selected observers were instructed to attempt to correctly identify as many of the national insignia as possible. Special emphasis was placed on the need to differentiate between US markings and those of other nations. At the time the 'white star on blue disc' (War Dept/Circular#141,)was the official insignia displayed on all AAF and US Navy warplanes. The results of these tests pointed out a definitive need to improve the 'quick recognition' characteristics of the existing insignia design. The answer was the addition of the 'bars' to the 'star and circle' design, a characteristic that has endured to current day US military aircraft. Although the graphics in the right hand column fall short of fully illustrating the problem of insignia recognition involving multiple aircraft traveling in excess of 150 miles per hour, it does present a general idea of the problem relating to instant identification faced by the AAF in early World War II.

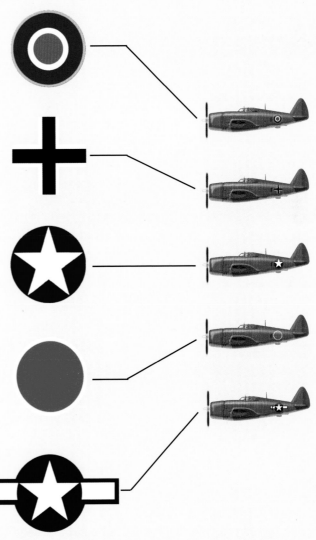

The following diagrams show the official WW II / USAAF specifications for placement of the national insignia and tail numbers as they applied to the fighter aircraft depicted. It is important to note that a combat aircraft might undergo any number of surface modifications, some of which would alter the original size and placement of the factory applications depicted on these diagrams. To those interested in a specific aircraft at a specific time in World War II, it is strongly suggested that a thorough study and comparative analysis of actual wartime photographs pertaining to that subject be conducted. Such research will often reveal variations in positioning, color and configuration of markings and paint schemes differing from those detailed in official USAAF or ANA directives. The three photographs in the adjacent column are included to address a marking scheme employed by the AAF prior to the outbreak of hostilities in 1941. These were colored cowling bands and fuselage command stripes. These devises were used to denote group, squadron and flight leaders but were not much used overseas. A few fighter units did utilize some form of command stripe during their wartime deployment , but these examples were rare. When applicable, and also confirmable, reference is made within this text to those groups/squadrons that employed such devices overseas regardless of how briefly.

LOCKHEED P-38 'LIGHTNING'

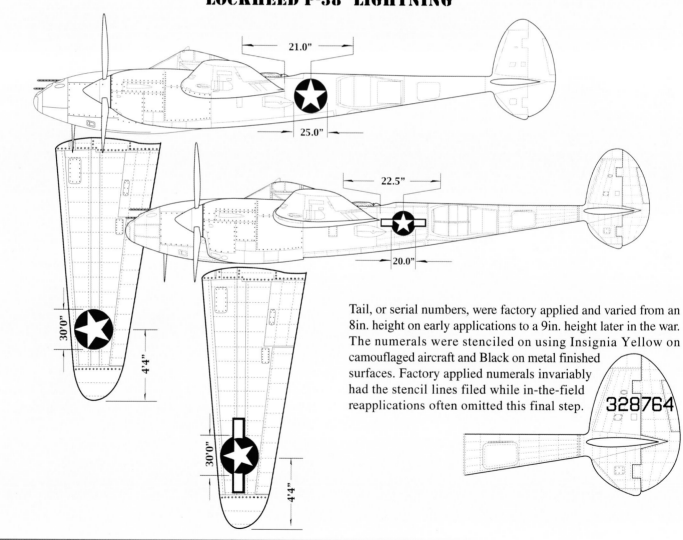

21.0"

25.0"

22.5"

20.0"

30'0"

4'4"

30'0"

4'4"

Tail, or serial numbers, were factory applied and varied from an 8in. height on early applications to a 9in. height later in the war. The numerals were stenciled on using Insignia Yellow on camouflaged aircraft and Black on metal finished surfaces. Factory applied numerals invariably had the stencil lines filed while in-the-field reapplications often omitted this final step.

328764

NORTH AMERICAN P-51 'MUSTANG'

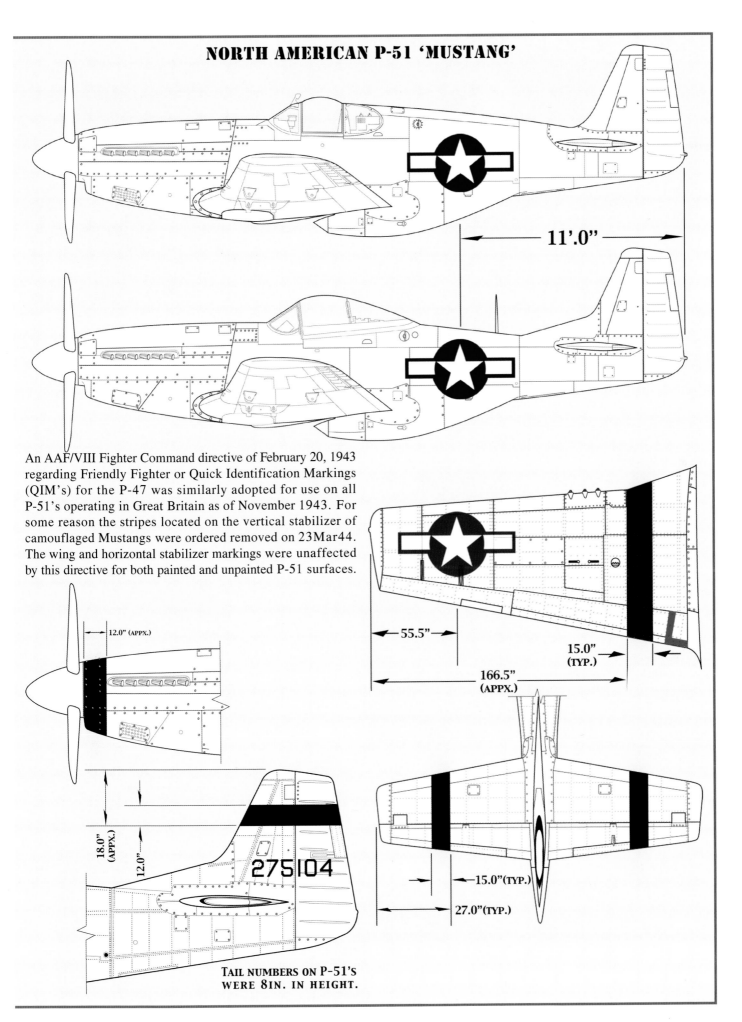

11'.0"

An AAF/VIII Fighter Command directive of February 20, 1943 regarding Friendly Fighter or Quick Identification Markings (QIM's) for the P-47 was similarly adopted for use on all P-51's operating in Great Britain as of November 1943. For some reason the stripes located on the vertical stabilizer of camouflaged Mustangs were ordered removed on 23Mar44. The wing and horizontal stabilizer markings were unaffected by this directive for both painted and unpainted P-51 surfaces.

12.0" (APPX.)

55.5"

15.0" (TYP.)

166.5" (APPX.)

18.0" (APPX.)

12.0"

275104

15.0"(TYP.)

27.0"(TYP.)

TAIL NUMBERS ON P-51'S WERE 8IN. IN HEIGHT.

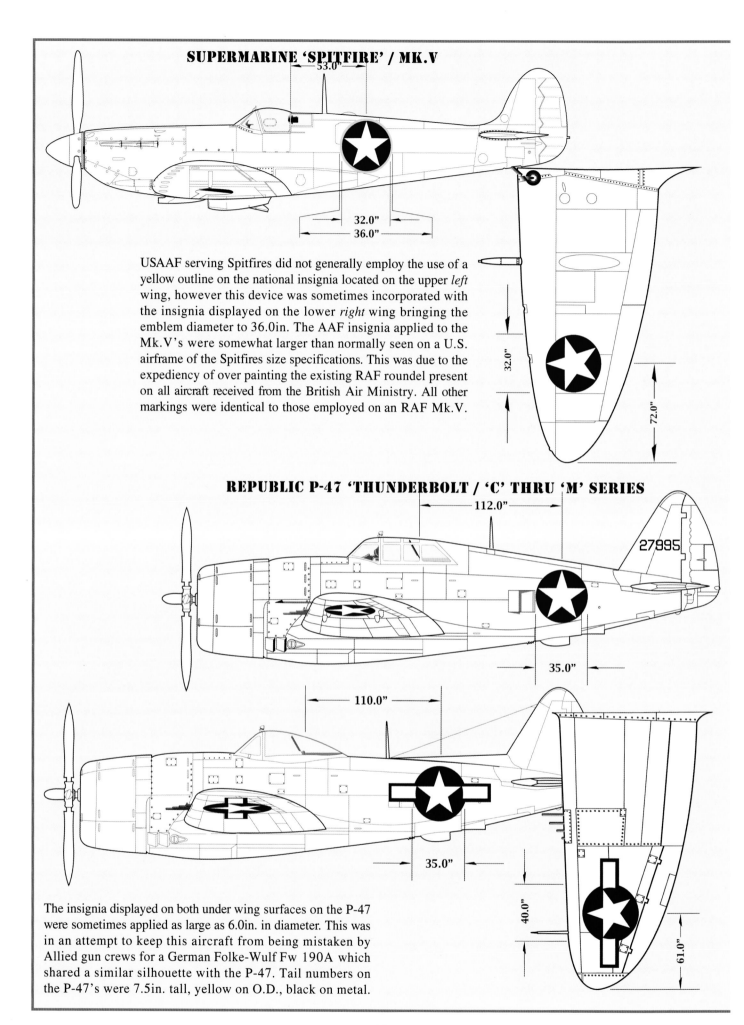

SUPERMARINE 'SPITFIRE' / MK.V

53.0"

32.0"
36.0"

32.0"

72.0"

USAAF serving Spitfires did not generally employ the use of a yellow outline on the national insignia located on the upper *left* wing, however this device was sometimes incorporated with the insignia displayed on the lower *right* wing bringing the emblem diameter to 36.0in. The AAF insignia applied to the Mk.V's were somewhat larger than normally seen on a U.S. airframe of the Spitfires size specifications. This was due to the expediency of over painting the existing RAF roundel present on all aircraft received from the British Air Ministry. All other markings were identical to those employed on an RAF Mk.V.

REPUBLIC P-47 'THUNDERBOLT / 'C' THRU 'M' SERIES

112.0"

27995

35.0"

110.0"

35.0"

40.0"

61.0"

The insignia displayed on both under wing surfaces on the P-47 were sometimes applied as large as 6.0in. in diameter. This was in an attempt to keep this aircraft from being mistaken by Allied gun crews for a German Folke-Wulf Fw 190A which shared a similar silhouette with the P-47. Tail numbers on the P-47's were 7.5in. tall, yellow on O.D., black on metal.

P-47 TAIL NUMBERS

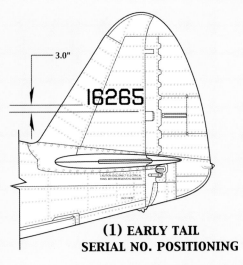

**(1) EARLY TAIL
SERIAL NO. POSITIONING**

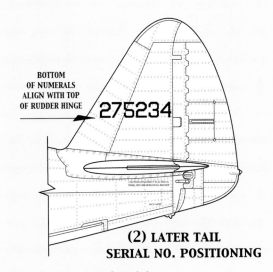

BOTTOM
OF NUMERALS
ALIGN WITH TOP
OF RUDDER HINGE

**(2) LATER TAIL
SERIAL NO. POSITIONING**

Increased wartime production resulted in higher aircraft serial numbers, and the addition of another digit to these numbers required a wider space than that of the original positioning (example 1). This minor space-fitting problem was solved by simply dropping the base line down three inches to align with the bottom of the central rudder hinge (example 2). The original location would have required a smaller stencil; this move negated a reduction in numeral size. Tail numbers (also referred to as call-numbers) were factory applied with yellow on standard camouflaged surfaces and black on metal finishes.

P-47 ALLIED EXPEDITIONARY AIR FORCE MARKINGS

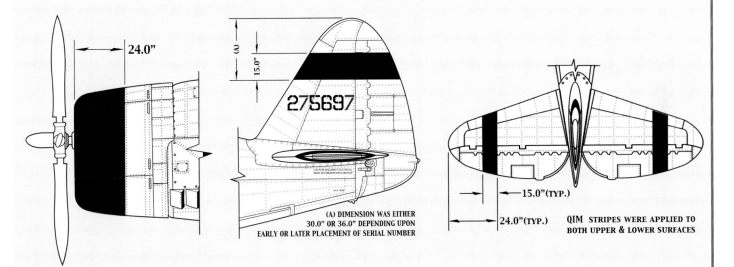

(A) DIMENSION WAS EITHER
30.0" OR 36.0" DEPENDING UPON
EARLY OR LATER PLACEMENT OF SERIAL NUMBER

QIM STRIPES WERE APPLIED TO
BOTH UPPER & LOWER SURFACES

These markings, also known as U.K. Special Recognition, Friendly Fighter and Quick Identification Markings, were adopted early in the original deployment of the U.S. Eighth Army Air Force to Great Britain. Due to a number of friendly fire incidents it was determined that an additional form of recognition was needed to assist Allied gun crews in differentiating between German and American fighter aircraft. The Thunderbolt, as previously stated, was often mistaken for a German Focke-Wulf Fw-190A while the P-51's were just as likely to be erroneously identified as a Mersserschmitt Bf 109.

It was the hope of both the British Air Ministry and AAF / VIII Fighter Command that these markings would alleviate many, if not most, of these 'mistaken identity' problems. There is no way of determining exactly how effective these QIM markings proved to be in reducing friendly fire mishaps. However, even though gradually phased out as the war progressed, a substantial number of 8th and 9th AAF fighter units continued to display these markings until the cession of hostilities. The standard application for the QIM's on these fighters was white on camouflaged surfaces and black on natural metal finishes.

ALLIED INVASION (D-DAY) STRIPES

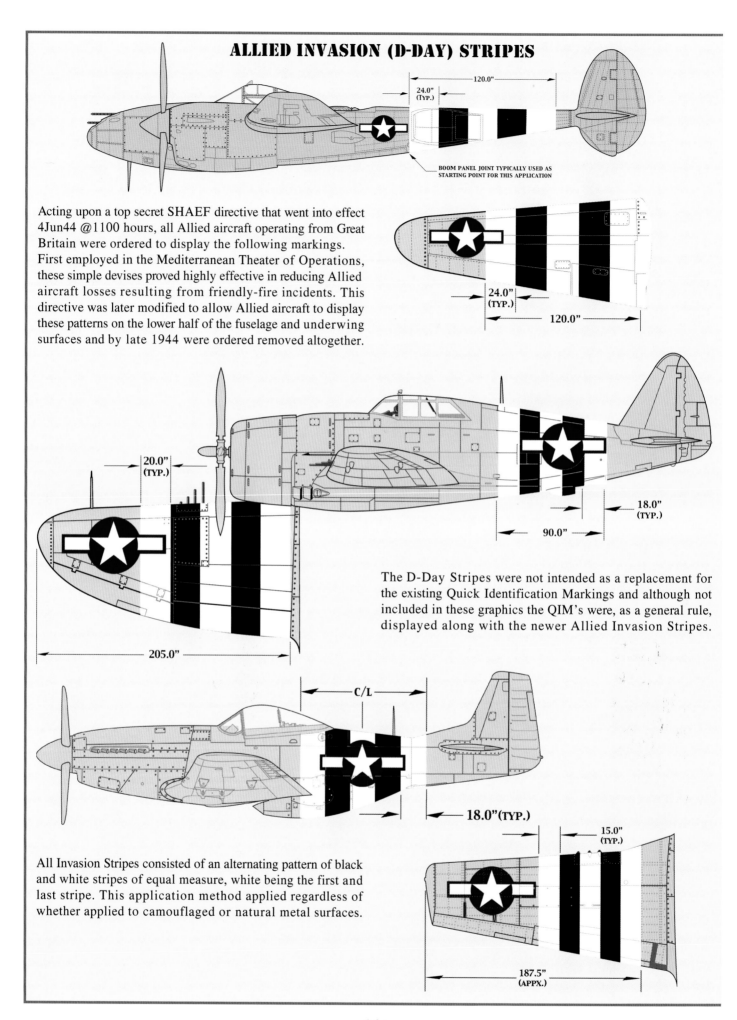

120.0"

24.0" (TYP.)

BOOM PANEL JOINT TYPICALLY USED AS
STARTING POINT FOR THIS APPLICATION

Acting upon a top secret SHAEF directive that went into effect 4Jun44 @1100 hours, all Allied aircraft operating from Great Britain were ordered to display the following markings. First employed in the Mediterranean Theater of Operations, these simple devises proved highly effective in reducing Allied aircraft losses resulting from friendly-fire incidents. This directive was later modified to allow Allied aircraft to display these patterns on the lower half of the fuselage and underwing surfaces and by late 1944 were ordered removed altogether.

24.0" (TYP.)

120.0"

20.0" (TYP.)

18.0" (TYP.)

90.0"

205.0"

The D-Day Stripes were not intended as a replacement for the existing Quick Identification Markings and although not included in these graphics the QIM's were, as a general rule, displayed along with the newer Allied Invasion Stripes.

C/L

18.0" (TYP.)

15.0" (TYP.)

187.5" (APPX.)

All Invasion Stripes consisted of an alternating pattern of black and white stripes of equal measure, white being the first and last stripe. This application method applied regardless of whether applied to camouflaged or natural metal surfaces.

* P-51 Nose Markings index

*Note: Some of the Groups listed above adopted one or more nose patterns while deployed in Great Britain. The configurations depicted on this page reflect the final patterns adopted by each Group prior to the end of World War II. Earlier patterns, including variations in color usage, are represented within each Groups respective section. Additionally, unit identifying characteristics employed on any combat aircraft other than the P-51 Mustang, when applicable, are similarly depicted.

* P-47 Nose Markings Index

56TH FIGHTER GROUP
PAGE 42

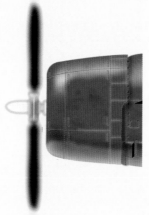

356TH FIGHTER GROUP
PAGE 68

78TH FIGHTER GROUP
PAGE 48

359TH FIGHTER GROUP
PAGE 78

353RD FIGHTER GROUP
PAGE 62

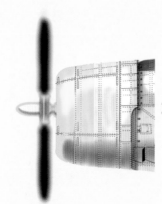

361ST FIGHTER GROUP
PAGE 82

*Note: Some of the Groups listed above adopted one or more nose patterns while deployed in Great Britain. The configurations depicted on this page reflect the final patterns adopted by each Group prior to the end of World War II. Earlier patterns, including variations in color usage, are represented within each Groups respective section. Additionally, unit identifying characteristics employed on any combat aircraft other than the P-47 Thunderbolt, when applicable, are similarly depicted.

This Index page is not inclusive as a of number of fighter groups assigned to the Eighth Army Air Force, in addition to those depicted above, conducted combat operations utilizing the Thunderbolt. Those Groups that did in fact operate the P-47 and are not listed above were omitted due to the fact that some units converted to the P-51 Mustang at a time when the dominant cowling identification devise in use was the 24 inch white UK/QIM band, prior to high profile Group markings.

8TH USAAF
FIGHTER GROUPS

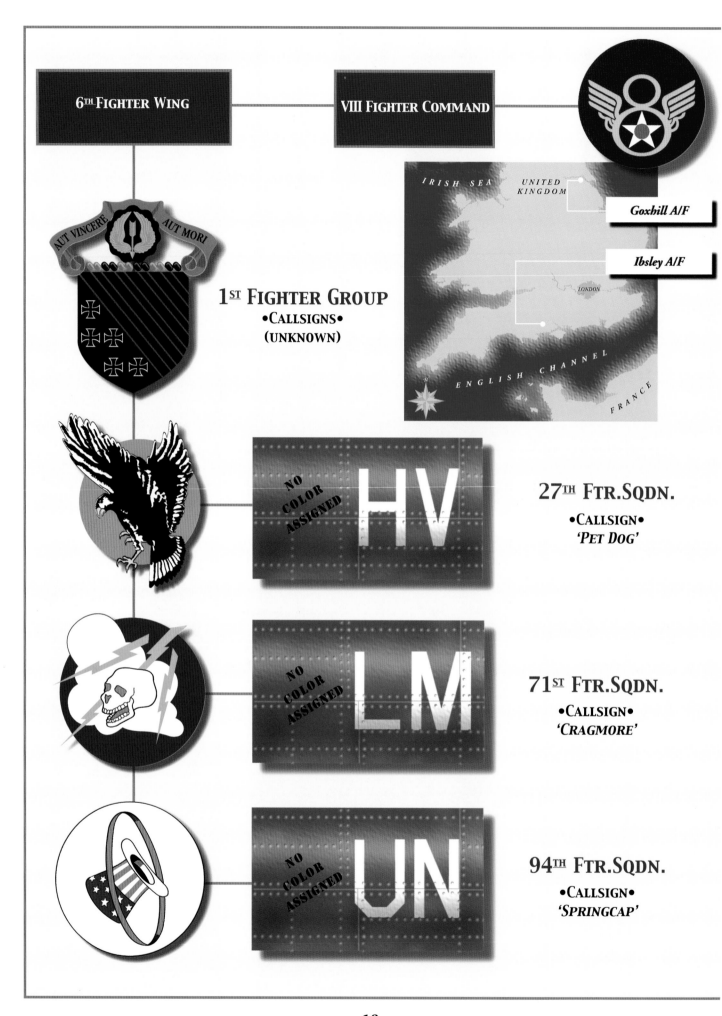

6TH FIGHTER WING

VIII FIGHTER COMMAND

Goxhill A/F

Ibsley A/F

IRISH SEA

UNITED KINGDOM

LONDON

ENGLISH CHANNEL

FRANCE

AUT VINCERE   AUT MORI

1ST FIGHTER GROUP
•CALLSIGNS•
(UNKNOWN)

NO COLOR ASSIGNED

HV

27TH FTR.SQDN.
•CALLSIGN•
'PET DOG'

NO COLOR ASSIGNED

LM

71ST FTR.SQDN.
•CALLSIGN•
'CRAGMORE'

NO COLOR ASSIGNED

UN

94TH FTR.SQDN.
•CALLSIGN•
'SPRINGCAP'

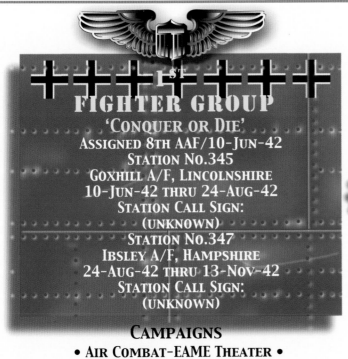

1st FIGHTER GROUP
'CONQUER OR DIE'
ASSIGNED 8TH AAF/10-JUN-42
STATION NO.345
GOXHILL A/F, LINCOLNSHIRE
10-JUN-42 THRU 24-AUG-42
STATION CALL SIGN:
(UNKNOWN)
STATION NO.347
IBSLEY A/F, HAMPSHIRE
24-AUG-42 THRU 13-NOV-42
STATION CALL SIGN:
(UNKNOWN)

CAMPAIGNS
- AIR COMBAT-EAME THEATER •
- AIR OFFENSIVE-EUROPE •
- ALGERIA-FRENCH MOROCCO • TUNISIA •
- SICILY • NAPLES-FOGGIA • ROME-ARNO •
- NORMANDY • NORTHERN FRANCE •
- SOUTHERN FRANCE • NORTH APENNINES •
- RHINELAND • CENTRAL EUROPE • PO VALLEY •

Although the 1stFG was assigned to the EighthAF for a very brief period, June thru November of 1942, it flew numerous combat sorties while so assigned before going on to serve with distinction with the 12th and later 15th AAFs'. Squadrons of the 1st Fighter Group received their overseas codes in Sep '42 and these were soon applied to all aircraft radiator housings in 18in. tall Sky or white letters. 'Plane-In-Group' assignment or 'Last Three' aircraft serial number digits sometimes adorned the fuselage nose or forward engine cowling area of 1stFG P-38s.

Of the three squadron insignia, the 27th FtrSqn was the only design with continuous longevity prior to WWII. Officially approved by the Army Board of Heraldry in 1924, this image can be traced back to WWI as the combat insignia for the 27th Aero Sqdn. The 'Indian Head' insignia below is actually the oldest of all these images. This symbol was originally the combat insignia of the Lafayette Escadrille, those young American pilots who flew for France prior to the United States entry into WWI. When ultimately transferred into the U.S. Army Air Service as the 103rd Aero Sqdn, this insignia went with them as that units insignia. The 103rd was subsequently consolidated with the 94th Aero Sqdn which had already adopted the 'Hat In The Ring' devise. This latter design was finally adopted as the official insignia of the 94th in 1919 only to again be replaced by the Indian Head motif in 1924. Just prior to the groups deployment overseas in 1942, former 94th Aero Sqdn Ace, Captain Eddie Rickenbacker successfully lobbied for the reinstatement of the 'Hat In The Ring' symbol as the official Group insignia of the 94th Fighter Squadron.

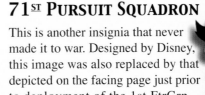

71ST PURSUIT SQUADRON

This is another insignia that never made it to war. Designed by Disney, this image was also replaced by that depicted on the facing page just prior to deployment of the 1st FtrGrp.

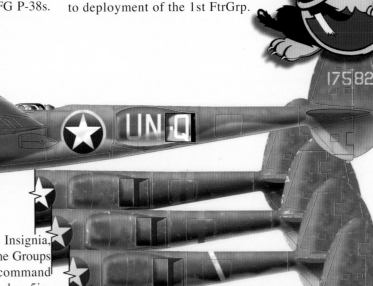

Other than the numerical markings and U.S. Type-2 Insignia, the only other distinguishing marks displayed by the Groups aircraft for its' first few months in the UK were 'command stripes' affixed to both tail booms. These were applied as 5in. encircling bands in respective squadron colors; twin bands for squadron COs', single bands for flight leaders. Use of these devices was discontinued with the adoption of letter codes.

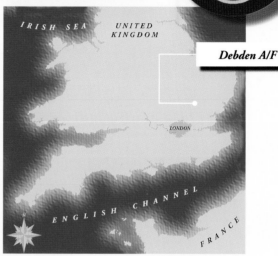

65ᵀᴴ FIGHTER WING — **2ᴺᴰ BOMBARDMENT (AIR) DIVISION** — **VIII FIGHTER COMMAND**

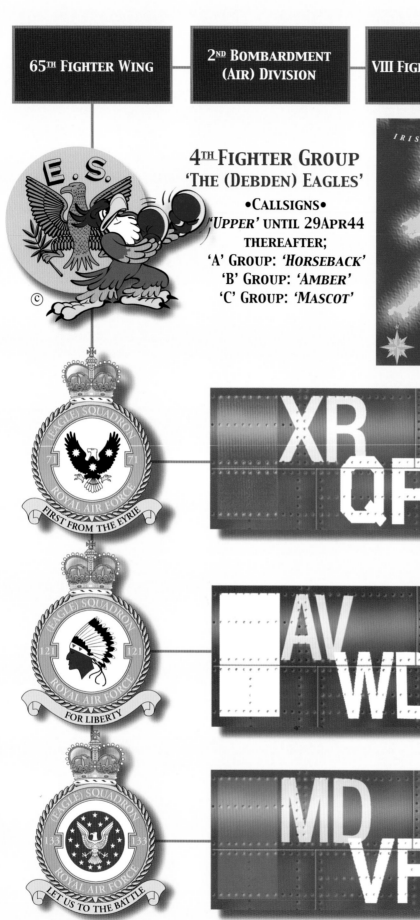

4ᵀᴴ FIGHTER GROUP
'THE (DEBDEN) EAGLES'

•CALLSIGNS•
'UPPER' UNTIL 29APR44
THEREAFTER;
'A' GROUP: 'HORSEBACK'
'B' GROUP: 'AMBER'
'C' GROUP: 'MASCOT'

Debden A/F

IRISH SEA
UNITED KINGDOM
LONDON
ENGLISH CHANNEL
FRANCE

334ᵀᴴ FIGHTER SQDN.
•CALLSIGNS•
'PECTIN' UNTIL 29APR44
THEREAFTER;
'A' GROUP: 'COBWEB'
'B' GROUP: 'TIFFIN'
'C' GROUP: (NONE)

335ᵀᴴ FIGHTER SQDN.
•CALLSIGNS•
'GREENBELT' UNTIL 29APR44
THEREAFTER;
'A' GROUP: 'CABOOSE'
'B' GROUP: 'SUPREME'
'C' GROUP: (NONE)

336ᵀᴴ FIGHTER SQDN.
•CALLSIGNS•
'SHIRTBLUE' UNTIL 29APR44
THEREAFTER;
'A' GROUP: 'BECKY'
'B' GROUP: 'RONNIE'
'C' GROUP: (NONE)

4TH FIGHTER GROUP
'FOURTH BUT FIRST'

ASSIGNED 8TH AAF/SEP'42
STATION NO.356
DEBDEN A/F, ESSEX
STATION CALLSIGN:
'CARMAN' UNTIL 29-APR-44
THEREAFTER, 'DICTON'

CAMPAIGNS
• AIR OFFENSIVE-EUROPE • NORMANDY •
• NORTHERN FRANCE • RHINELAND •
• ARDENNES-ALSACE • CENTRAL EUROPE •

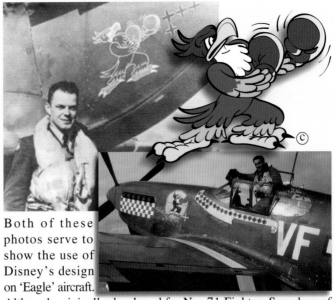

Both of these photos serve to show the use of Disney's design on 'Eagle' aircraft. Although originally developed for No. 71 Fighter Squadron of the RAF, it enjoyed wide use within the other two American Volunteer units as well. When all three Eagle Squadrons were transferred to the USAAF, this same design became the unofficial combat insignia for the newly formed 4th Fighter Group.

The squadron insignia depicted on the facing page were in fact approved by the British Air Ministry for Americans serving in No's. 71, 121 and 133 'Eagle' Squadrons of the RAF. These insignia continued to be displayed by each respective squadron long after their transfer to the US Army Air Force. The images at left represent the RAF insignia under which these Eagle pilots served.

These graphics depict variations of the original Disney design and became synonymous with 'The Eagles' throughout the war years. The lower of these two was officially readopted as the insignia of the 334th Fighter Squadron in 1950.

The original **X R / A V / M D** codes which had been carried over from the squadrons RAF days were replaced in early April '43 with the now familiar **Q P / W D / M D** designations.

After assimilation into the U.S.A.A.F., the wearing of the British Pilots Wings over the right pocket of the US dress uniform was a unique source of pride for those select few who had the distinction of having flown with the former Eagle Squadrons.

Although reportedly developed for the unit prior to the end of WWII, this image was not *officially* adopted by the 4th FtrGrp until September of 1949 at which time the former Army Air Force had evolved into the present United States Air Force. Although this design lacks the units former 'Eagle' image, the groups ties to the United Kingdom are nonetheless well represented by the symbolic indomitable British Lion surmounting the crest.

'SPITFIRE' MK. VB
C. SEP'42-APR'43

For over six months after transferring to the USAAF, the former Eagle Squadron pilots continued to fly their familiar Mk.Vb Spitfire's. These were to retain the original RAF Temperate Zone camouflage paint scheme consisting of an Ocean Grey and Dark Green top surface over a Medium Sea Grey.

An additional 'friendlies' recognition element was added to the rear fuselage area of all 4thFG Spits. This consisted of an 18in wide band of color applied with RAF Sky Blue. The original fuselage identification number was often over painted and not subsequently reinstated. The squadron codes originally approved for the three Eagle Squadrons by the British Air Ministry were temporarily adopted by the group and applied in letter cap heights varying from between 24 and 30 inches in an RAF Sky Blue.

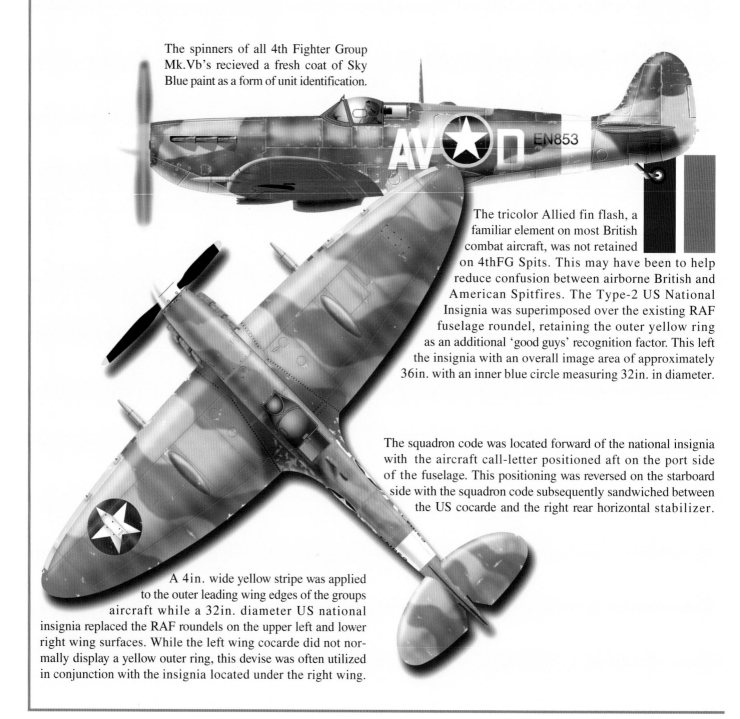

The spinners of all 4th Fighter Group Mk.Vb's recieved a fresh coat of Sky Blue paint as a form of unit identification.

The tricolor Allied fin flash, a familiar element on most British combat aircraft, was not retained on 4thFG Spits. This may have been to help reduce confusion between airborne British and American Spitfires. The Type-2 US National Insignia was superimposed over the existing RAF fuselage roundel, retaining the outer yellow ring as an additional 'good guys' recognition factor. This left the insignia with an overall image area of approximately 36in. with an inner blue circle measuring 32in. in diameter.

The squadron code was located forward of the national insignia with the aircraft call-letter positioned aft on the port side of the fuselage. This positioning was reversed on the starboard side with the squadron code subsequently sandwiched between the US cocarde and the right rear horizontal stabilizer.

A 4in. wide yellow stripe was applied to the outer leading wing edges of the groups aircraft while a 32in. diameter US national insignia replaced the RAF roundels on the upper left and lower right wing surfaces. While the left wing cocarde did not normally display a yellow outer ring, this devise was often utilized in conjunction with the insignia located under the right wing.

P-47 'THUNDERBOLT'
C. MAR'43-FEB'44

The entire inventory of original 'C' Series P-47s allocated to the 4th FG arrived with a factory applied two-color camouflage paint scheme. This Olive Drab over Neutral Grey would continue to be the standard for all the Groups P-47s including the later 'D' Series which began arriving in June 1943. No natural metal finish Thunderbolts are known to have ever served with the 4thFG.

For a brief period lasting little more than two months (C. Feb-Apr '43) the 4thFG adopted a temporary system for identifying its' aircraft. The last two digits of the tail number were affixed to the fuselage forward the national insignia which at this time displayed a 2in. yellow surround. The Eighth A.A.F. directive specified these codes be applied in white paint with an overall height of twenty inches. All 4th FG aircraft at this time displayed standard white Q.I.M.'s.

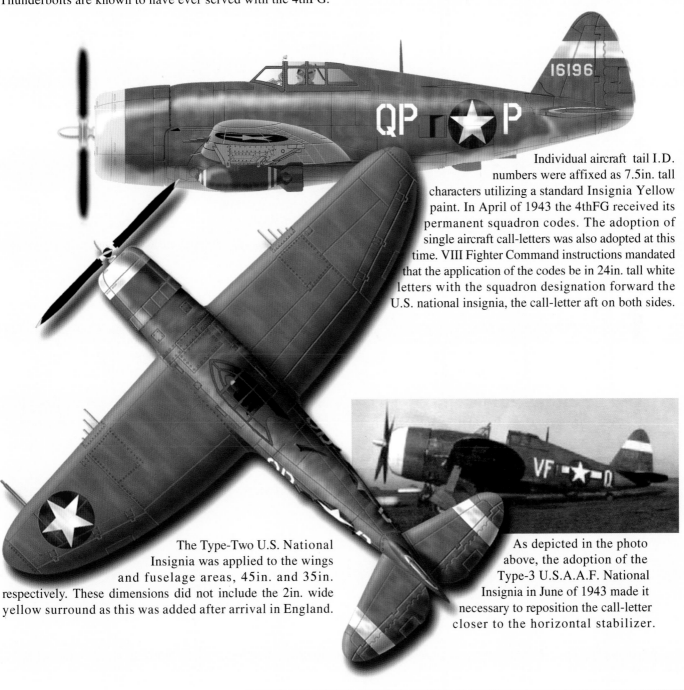

Individual aircraft tail I.D. numbers were affixed as 7.5in. tall characters utilizing a standard Insignia Yellow paint. In April of 1943 the 4thFG received its permanent squadron codes. The adoption of single aircraft call-letters was also adopted at this time. VIII Fighter Command instructions mandated that the application of the codes be in 24in. tall white letters with the squadron designation forward the U.S. national insignia, the call-letter aft on both sides.

The Type-Two U.S. National Insignia was applied to the wings and fuselage areas, 45in. and 35in. respectively. These dimensions did not include the 2in. wide yellow surround as this was added after arrival in England.

As depicted in the photo above, the adoption of the Type-3 U.S.A.A.F. National Insignia in June of 1943 made it necessary to reposition the call-letter closer to the horizontal stabilizer.

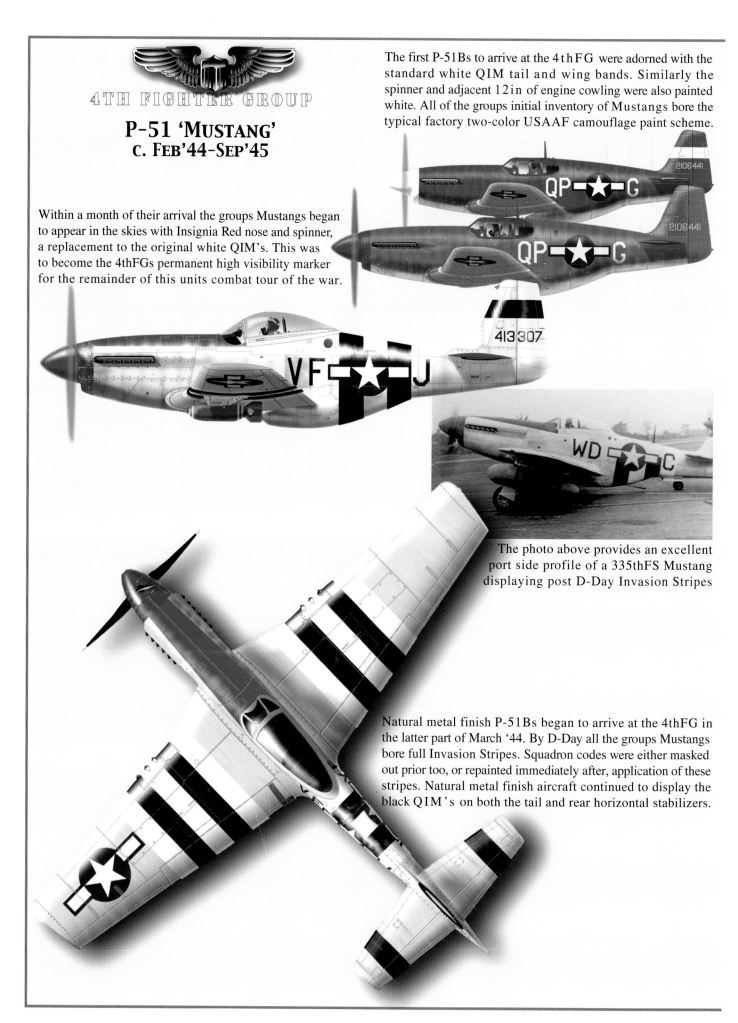

4TH FIGHTER GROUP

P-51 'MUSTANG'
c. FEB'44–SEP'45

The first P-51Bs to arrive at the 4th FG were adorned with the standard white QIM tail and wing bands. Similarly the spinner and adjacent 12in of engine cowling were also painted white. All of the groups initial inventory of Mustangs bore the typical factory two-color USAAF camouflage paint scheme.

Within a month of their arrival the groups Mustangs began to appear in the skies with Insignia Red nose and spinner, a replacement to the original white QIM's. This was to become the 4thFGs permanent high visibility marker for the remainder of this units combat tour of the war.

The photo above provides an excellent port side profile of a 335thFS Mustang displaying post D-Day Invasion Stripes

Natural metal finish P-51Bs began to arrive at the 4thFG in the latter part of March '44. By D-Day all the groups Mustangs bore full Invasion Stripes. Squadron codes were either masked out prior too, or repainted immediately after, application of these stripes. Natural metal finish aircraft continued to display the black QIM's on both the tail and rear horizontal stabilizers.

24

4TH FIGHTER GROUP

In early December, 1944, it was decided to extend the existing Insignia Red an additional 12in. further back on the engine cowling. This modification brought the rearward edge of the color band to a point approximately just aft the second exhaust port.

Sometime in the summer of 1944, the 334thFS began applying squadron codes and call-letters to a number of their aircraft using a thin red outline. The 336thFS followed suit by incorporating a red drop-shadow with its fuselage applications and in fact, by wars end, each respective squadron had unofficially adopted an individualized style of aircraft letter.

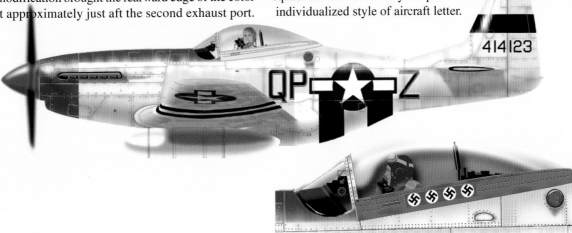

Due to a developing problem in differentiating 4th Fighter Group aircraft from similarly marked units within other U.S. Army Air Forces a new 'sweep' nose paint application was adopted in early January 1945. As the war neared its end, fighter groups once separated by literally thousands of miles, now found themselves operating in much greater proximity to one another. The similar color schemes employed by several individual squadrons began to result in erroneous allied unit identification reports.

Although never officially approved or universally adopted within the 4thFG, numerous individual aircraft within the unit had the main canopy frame painted in a respective squadron color.

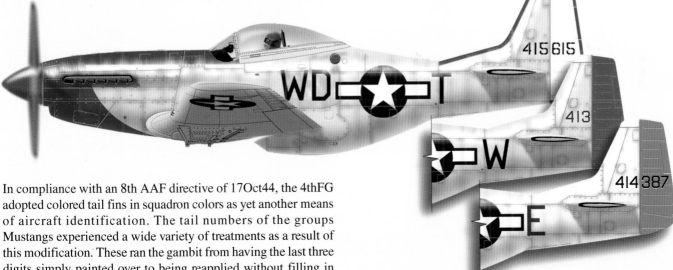

In compliance with an 8th AAF directive of 17Oct44, the 4thFG adopted colored tail fins in squadron colors as yet another means of aircraft identification. The tail numbers of the groups Mustangs experienced a wide variety of treatments as a result of this modification. These ran the gambit from having the last three digits simply painted over to being reapplied without filling in stencil lines. Some numbers were fully restored to original specs while others were removed from the tail section altogether.

To further assist in recognition, 335thFS often outlined the tail and rudder with a red stripe, usually 1 to 2 inches in width. The 'medium blue' rudders of 336thFS Mustangs varied in shade from one aircraft to another and was possibly due to using what was available at any given time. Some applications were actually quite dark in value and appear to have been a mix of the Insignia Blue and white paint such as used for the Type-3 USAAF markings. The black rudder stripes were dropped at this time as were those on the horizontal stabilizers the following year (March, 1945).

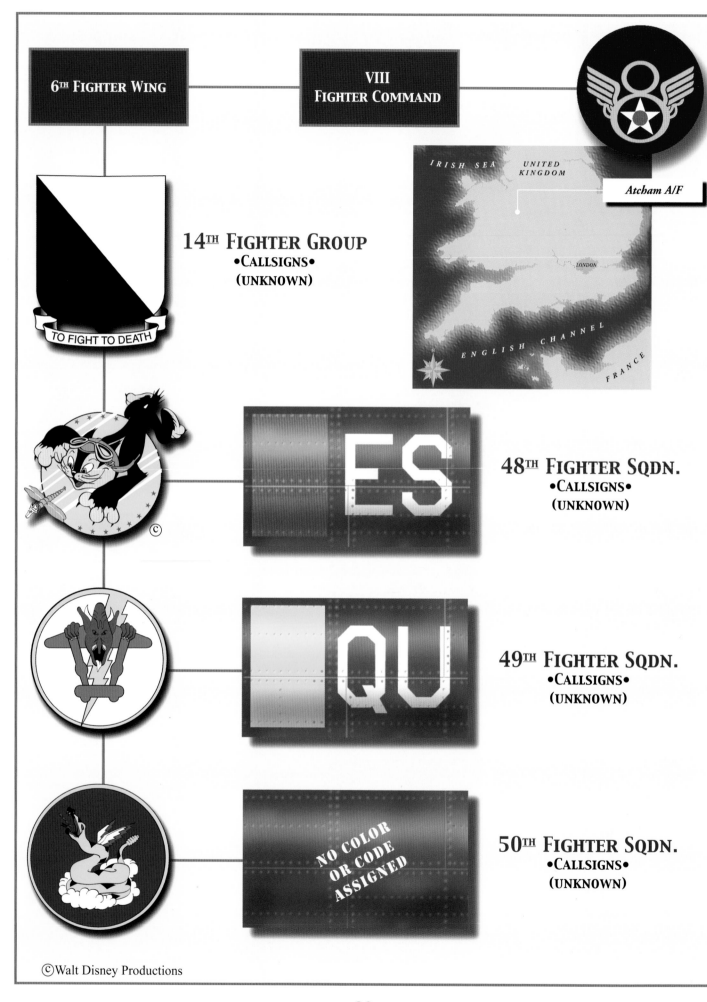

6TH FIGHTER WING

VIII FIGHTER COMMAND

IRISH SEA
UNITED KINGDOM

Atcham A/F

LONDON

ENGLISH CHANNEL

FRANCE

14TH FIGHTER GROUP
•CALLSIGNS•
(UNKNOWN)

TO FIGHT TO DEATH

48TH FIGHTER SQDN.
•CALLSIGNS•
(UNKNOWN)

ES

49TH FIGHTER SQDN.
•CALLSIGNS•
(UNKNOWN)

QU

50TH FIGHTER SQDN.
•CALLSIGNS•
(UNKNOWN)

NO COLOR OR CODE ASSIGNED

14TH FIGHTER GROUP

'To Fight To Death'
ASSIGNED 8TH AAF
18-AUG-42 THRU 15-NOV-42
STATION No.342
ATCHAM A/F, SHROPSHIRE
STATION CALLSIGN:
(UNKNOWN)

CAMPAIGNS

- AIR COMBAT, EAME THEATER •
- AIR OFFENSIVE-EUROPE •
- AIR OFFENSIVE, EUROPE • TUNISIA •
- SICILY • NAPLES-FOGGIA • ROME-ARNO •
- NORMANDY • NORTHERN FRANCE •
- SOUTHERN FRANCE • NORTH APENNINES •
- RHINELAND • CENTRAL EUROPE • PO VALLEY •

The 14th Fighter Group was another unit whose tenure with the 8th USAAF was brief and in fact did not survive its deployment to the UK intact. While enroute to England the 50th FS was held over in Iceland and destined never to be reunited with the 14th. The 50th was ultimately replaced by the 37th Fighter Squadron in March 1943, some time after the groups transfer to North Africa with the 15th Air Force.

A note concerning the squadron insignia; The 48th Fighter Squadron image depicted on the preceding page was designed by Disney Studios when that unit still carried a Pursuit Squadron designation (pre'42). It is believed that this image remained in the States when the group shipped out. At the time of this writing it is unknown what insignia, if any, replaced it during the war. The insignia for the 49th was never officially approved but was nevertheless displayed by this squadron for the majority of its combat tour. Ironically, the only official wartime combat insignia was that of the orphaned 50th Fighter Squadron which had been approved by the Army in April 1942, just in time for the 48th FGs' overseas deployment four months later.

The 14th Fighter Group P-38Fs utilized Command Stripes on their aircrafts boom area. The commanding officers ship bore twin 5"in wide Insignia Red vertical bands aft the radiator housing area. Flight commanders aircraft carried a single vertical stripe in the same location each with their respective squadron color.

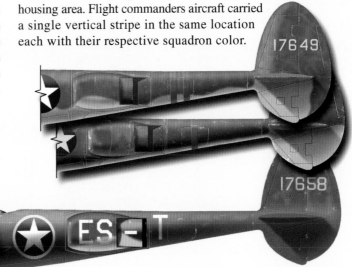

The 48th and 49th were assigned their squadron codes while with the 8th A.F. and participated in a number of combat sorties, these being primarily fighter sweeps along the French coastline. For the most part these codes were applied as 20in. tall block letters in RAF Sky Blue but there were numerous variations to this rule throughout the group. Some aircraft within both squadrons even received a contour outline of Insignia Yellow to complement the Sky Blue letters.

67TH FIGHTER WING	1ST BOMBARDMENT (AIR) DIVISION	VIII FIGHTER COMMAND

20TH FIGHTER GROUP
'THE LOCO BUSTERS'
•CALLSIGNS•
'DENTON' UNTIL 22-APR-44
THEREAFTER
'A' GROUP: 'WALNUT'
'B' GROUP: 'OATMEAL'
'C' GROUP: 'KATIE'

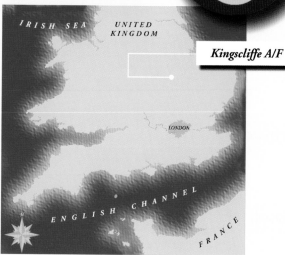

Kingscliffe A/F

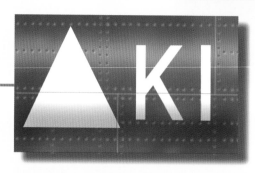

55TH FIGHTER SQDN.
•CALLSIGNS•
'TOWNTALK' UNTIL 22-APR-44
THEREAFTER
'A' GROUP: 'SAILOR'
'B' GROUP: 'PATOR'
'C' GROUP: (NONE)

77TH FIGHTER SQDN.
•CALLSIGNS•
'REBUKE' UNTIL 22-APR-44
THEREAFTER
'A' GROUP: 'OUTCRY'
'B' GROUP: 'GLORY'
'C' GROUP: (NONE)

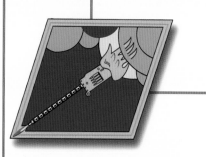

79TH FIGHTER SQDN.
•CALLSIGNS•
'CROWNWRIGHT' UNTIL 22-APR-44
THEREAFTER
'A' GROUP: 'PRIMROSE'
'B' GROUP: 'SCREWGUN'
'C' GROUP: (NONE)

20TH FIGHTER GROUP

'VICTORY BY VALOR'

ASSIGNED 8TH AAF/25-AUG-43
STATION NO.367
KINGS CLIFFE A/F, NORTHAMPTONSHIRE
C.26-AUG-43 THRU C.11-OCT-45
STATION CALL SIGN:
'CHURCHPATH'

CAMPAIGNS
- AMERICAN THEATER •
- AIR OFFENSIVE-EUROPE •
- NORMANDY • NORTHERN FRANCE •
- RHINELAND • ARDENNES-ALSACE •
- CENTRAL EUROPE •

This is an interesting photo in that it illustrates the use of the 77th FS insignia. In addition to the ready room entrance sign, note the 77th patch on the flight jacket.

With the adoption of the new geometric pattern squadron tail markers, the aircraft ID numbers were often over-painted. This led to the application of the last three digits of those numbers to the nose section of the P-38s. These were stenciled using yellow on camouflaged and black on metal finished aircraft and positioned over the original contractors number. The stencil break lines on the nine inch tall letters were seldom filled in on these particular applications.

The combat insignia displayed by the 20th Fighter Group during the course of World War II originated in the 1930's and were authorized by the Army. Approval dates were 18Dec32 for the group insignia, 4May32 and 29Aug31 for the 55th and 77th Fighter Squadrons respectively. The insignia of the 79th Fighter Squadron was of bit younger in origin and not officially sanctioned until a little over a decade later, 31Jan43. For whatever reason, the 20th Fighter Group never utilized any squadron colors but opted instead to finish the war with the geometric tail symbols originally adopted in January, 1944.

The squadrons of the 20th Fighter Group were arguably the most prolific users of 'mission' symbols within 8th AAF Fighter Command. If the 20th didn't invent the use of these images, its squadrons certainly developed their application to a near art form. Whereas these two photos only show the use of these symbols on natural metal finished P-38s, they were also very much in evidence on the groups camouflaged Lightnings in addition to the units later P-51 Mustangs.

P-38 'LIGHTNING'
C. DEC'43-JUL'44

The 'Loco Busters' as the 20th Fighter Group would come to be known, underwent T/O training with Series 'H' P-38s and numerous pilots from all three squadrons flew missions with the 55th Fighter Group during the month of November. As the 55th was by that time operational, this allowed 20thFG flyers to gain some hands-on combat experience while awaiting receipt of their own allotment of current model combat aircraft.

Squadrons of the 20thFG were assigned their codes in October of 1943. During this time the application of P-38 code letters was standardized and called for the individual aircraft call-letter to be located centrally on the radiator housing while the squadron codes were positioned aft the radiator vent door. Specifications called for typical white 18in. tall block characters. A character width of 9in. was also called for but this varied somewhat in actual application. Geometric symbols, approximately 30in at their widest measure, were adopted by all three squadrons in January, 1944. These markers were applied with white paint to the groups existing inventory of camouflaged aircraft. Within a month the 20thFG began to receive metal finished 'J ' Series P-38s and these symbols would be affixed to these aircraft with black paint.

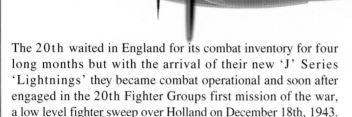

The 20th waited in England for its combat inventory for four long months but with the arrival of their new 'J' Series 'Lightnings' they became combat operational and soon after engaged in the 20th Fighter Groups first mission of the war, a low level fighter sweep over Holland on December 18th, 1943.

During the first few weeks of operation none of the 20thFG squadrons payed much attention to either the appearance or presence of individual aircraft tail numbers. If a given aircraft received a replacement tail rudder or simple routine painting maintenance, the original factory applied serial number was quite frequently not reinstated. This situation continued, albeit briefly, after the groups squadrons adopted their new geometric identification symbols, and for a time the tail number was simply over-painted.

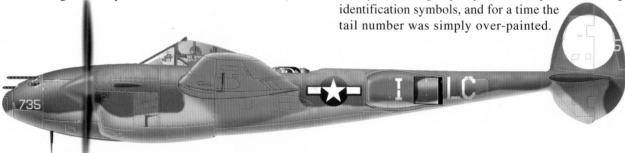

Note the tail sections of both these aircraft. The serial number on the camouflaged 55thFS ship at left has been fully reinstated after the addition of that units triangular identity symbol. In the example below, the serial number has been masked out with a solid stripe prior to the application of the 77thFS circle marker.

With the introduction of the Invasion Stripes immediately prior to the Normandy landings, both the squadron call-letter and the individual aircraft call-letter were over-painted. No attempt was made to mask-out these images before application of these stripes, neither were these codes reinstated after the stripes were applied. The commonly accepted practice among all 8th Army Air Force units flying P-38s was to relocate the aircraft call-letter to the inward facing sides of both vertical tail fins.

The group began receiving natural metal finished 'J' Series ' in February 1944. By early spring the practice of masking out a horizontal band directly over the existing a/c tail number had become an accepted practice within the all squadrons of the 20thFG. Aircraft whose tail numbers had previously been over-painted had those numbers reinstated, however in some instances the stencil lines of the reapplied numbers remained unpainted. Camouflaged aircraft whose tail numbers had previously been over-painted would have those numbers reinstated over the existing solid white geometric squadron markers. The horizontal masking technique employed with the metal finished aircraft was not utilized in the case of these camouflaged 'Lightnings'.

The new letters varied in size but were as a rule considerably larger than the ships original call-letters. In most cases the replacement images were nearly twice the size of the originals. There were those few applications however where the original 19in. fuselage stencils were utilized.

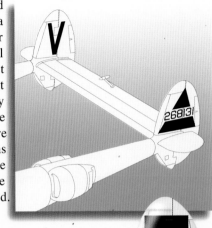

In March of 1944 the 20thFG adopted the color yellow as an additional means of unit recognition. This was applied to both of the aircrafts spinners as well as to the first 12 inches of the engine cowling, bringing the color band to a point immediately forward of the cowling air intake fairings. No other color markings were employed by the group on any of their P-38s.

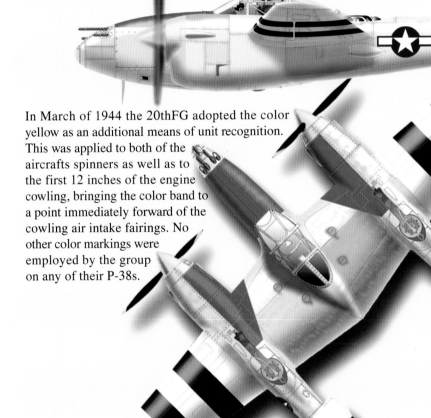

The application of mission panels to aircraft among the squadrons of the 20thFG was a wide spread custom. These symbols more often than not could be attributed to those missions conducted by the aircrafts primary pilot rather than the aircraft itself. It was common practice to 'loan' a ship to another flyer if his regularly assigned aircraft was undergoing maintenance and/or repairs. Those missions flown by the quest pilot would ultimately be affixed to his permanent aircraft and not the 'borrowed' ship actually used to perform those missions.

20TH FIGHTER GROUP

P-51 'MUSTANG'
c. JUL'44-SEP'45

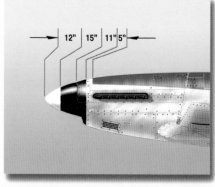

With the transition to P-51s, the 20thFG adopted a nose pattern like that depicted in this illustration. While it may have lacked some of the style and pizzazz exhibited by other 8thAAF Fighter Groups at this same time, it was none-the-less an early attempt to provide the groups aircraft with some means of an improved 'friendly forces' recognition factor. This pattern would only be in use by the 20thFG until November 1944 when it was replaced with the higher profile configuration depicted on the facing page.

All 'D' Series Mustangs delivered to the 20thFtrGrp were in natural metal finishes and were immediately adorned with full Invasion Stripes. The squadron code and aircraft call-letter on the fuselage remained of standard size and location and were either masked-out prior to application of these stripes or reinstated shortly thereafter. The respective geometric squadron symbol was affixed to either side of the fin and rudder area of all group fighters with black paint. Added to this squadron marker was a 30in. tall white call letter which had previously been located on the inward facing fin surfaces of the groups original P-38s.

Some of the 20thFG P-51s received an application of dark green paint to the entire upper surface of both wings and rear stabilizers. Additionally an 'edging' to the top surface of the entire fuselage and tail section was also applied. This was not an Olive Drab shade of green and was possibly something acquired from the RAF The rational behind this application was likely motivated by an anticipated deployment of elements of the 20thFG to the European continent subsequent to the D-Day landings. Whatever the reason, use of this color scheme had all but disappeared from virtually all of the 20th Fighter Group Mustangs by late 1944.

The black QIMs on both top wing surfaces disappeared with the application of the D-Day Stripes, while those stripes on the upper surface of the horizontal stabilizers were mostly over-painted when the green paint was applied.

These bands were however retained on a few of the groups camou-flaged aircraft. Those QIMs located on the under wing surfaces remained intact. Depending upon the individual application to the tail section, the QIM there might or might not have been retained. QIMs remained standard markings for all unpainted Mustangs.

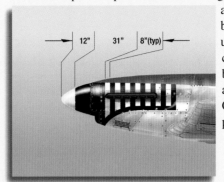

20TH FIGHTER GROUP

The second group nose pattern more-or-less picked up where the previous design had left off. With the exception of the spinner tip (which was either painted white or remained in a natural metal state) the remainder of this surface, in addition to the first 16in. (approximate) of the engine cowling were painted black. An alternating pattern of seven, eight inch black & white vertical stripes comprised the new configuration. As seen in the adjacent diagram, the bars (stripes) emanated upwards from a diagonal curved to horizontal black bar, terminating at the junction of the Olive Drab antiglare panel atop the fuselage.

In November of 1944 a new nose marking configuration was adopted by the 20th Fighter Group. This new design was a major improvement over the original pattern in assisting with aircraft unit identification. The surface area of the forward fuselage necessary to accommodate this new marking all but eliminated the application of the groups traditional 'mission tally panels' and these once familiar symbols became a rarity after this date. The black & white D-Day Invasion Stripes, which by now had been reduced to the lower surface areas in compliance with the 8th AAF directive, were themselves removed from virtually all the groups combat aircraft by years end. The original Quick Identification Markers on the wing and tail surfaces were not ordered to be removed but not applied to replacement aircraft .

All squadrons within the 20thFG adopted the use of adding a bar below an aircrafts call letter if that aircraft was the second within their respective unit to carry a duplicate call letter. This bar was displayed on both the ships fuselage as well as tail call letter locations.

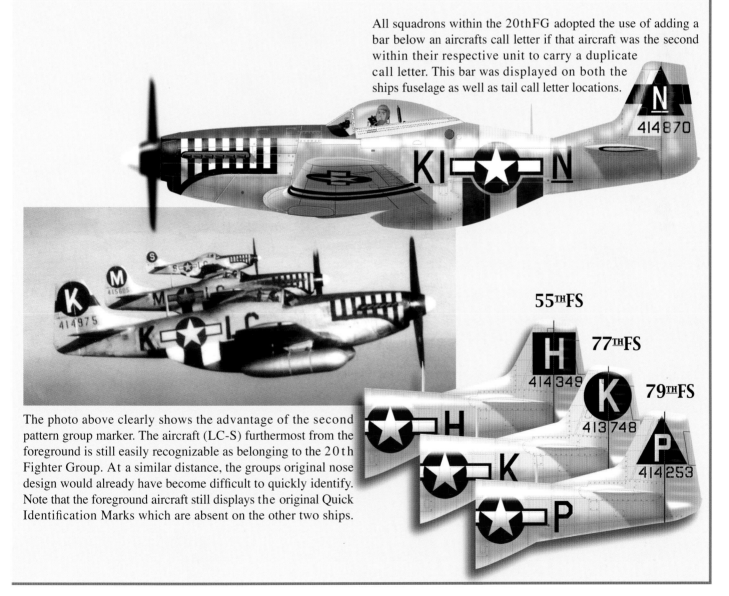

The photo above clearly shows the advantage of the second pattern group marker. The aircraft (LC-S) furthermost from the foreground is still easily recognizable as belonging to the 20th Fighter Group. At a similar distance, the groups original nose design would already have become difficult to quickly identify. Note that the foreground aircraft still displays the original Quick Identification Marks which are absent on the other two ships.

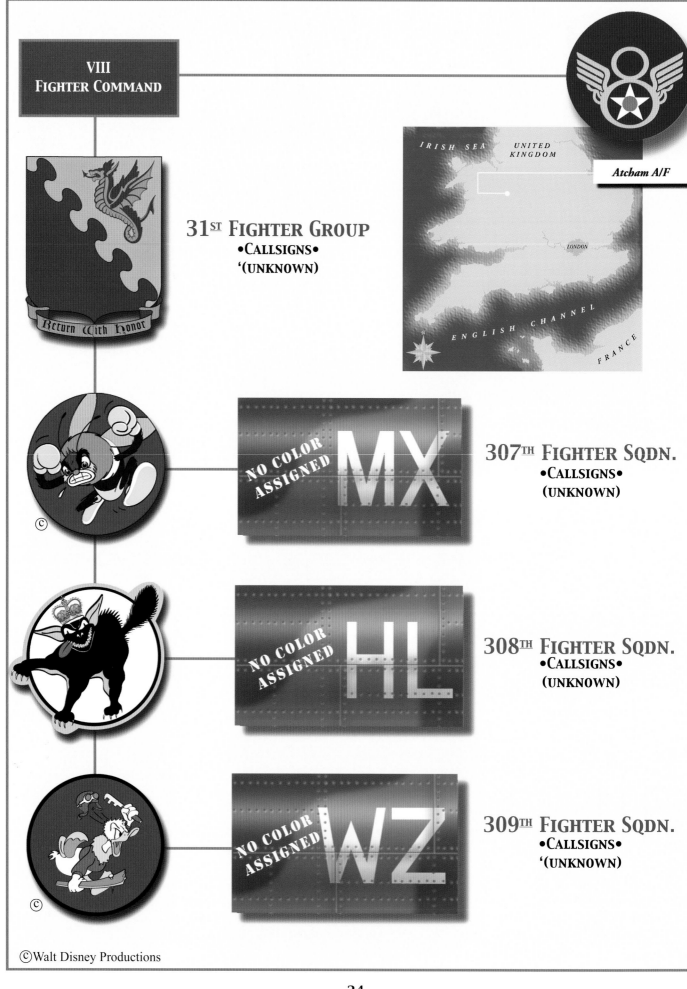

VIII FIGHTER COMMAND

31ST FIGHTER GROUP
•CALLSIGNS•
'(UNKNOWN)

Atcham A/F

IRISH SEA · UNITED KINGDOM

LONDON

ENGLISH CHANNEL · FRANCE

307TH FIGHTER SQDN.
•CALLSIGNS•
(UNKNOWN)

NO COLOR ASSIGNED — **MX**

308TH FIGHTER SQDN.
•CALLSIGNS•
(UNKNOWN)

NO COLOR ASSIGNED — **HL**

309TH FIGHTER SQDN.
•CALLSIGNS•
'(UNKNOWN)

NO COLOR ASSIGNED — **WZ**

FIGHTER GROUP
'Return With Honor'
Assigned 8th AAF/11-Jun-42
Station No.342
***Atcham A/F, Shropeshire**
c.11-Jun-42 thru c.1-Aug-42
Station Call sign:
(Unknown)
Station No.352
West Hampnett A/F, Sussex
c.1-Aug-42 thru c.7-Nov-42
Station Call Sigh:
(Unknown)

CAMPAIGNS
- Air Combat-EAME Theater •
- Air Offensive-Europe •
- Algeria-French Morocco • Tunisia • Sicily •
- Naples-Foggia • Anzio • Rome-Arno •
- Normandy • Northern France •
- Southern France • North Appines •
- Rhineland • Central Europe • Po Valley •

The adjacent insignia was a prewar Disney design and represented the 308th Fighter Squadron prior to deployment of the 31st Fighter Group to Merry Old England. This is yet another example of a stateside unit insignia being replaced by another image once actual combat operations commenced. The reason for doing away with the little Trojan design is uncertain today. Its demise may have been the need for a more aggressive image or simply that the C/O of the 308thFS wasn't a fan of the University of Southern California.

This is reputed to be a later variation of the 308thFS insignia represented on the facing page. At the time this work was ready for press, the actual use of this image by the 308thFS had not been unquestionably authenticated. It is the insignia often used today for representing this unit, thus its inclusion within this text.

For the brief period of time that the 31stFG was attached to the 8th Air Force it was nevertheless issued squadron codes which remained with the unit throughout the course of the war. The Mk.V Spitfires the group flew while with the Eighth displayed these codes in RAF Sky (Blue) forward the roundel on the port side of the aircraft fuselage, aft on the starboard side. The reverse applied to the placement of the aircraft call-letters. Letters were roughly 24in. in height.

The same friendly forces marking scheme used by the 4th Fighter Group (also equipped with British Spirfires) was employed by the 31stFG. As with the 4thFG, the tricolored panel was removed from the tail sections of all 31st FG Mk.Vb's as were most of the original RAF fuselage numbers.

The photograph above of the 309th FS pilots was actually taken in 1942 at La Senia, Algeria shortly after assignment of the 31stFG to the 12thAAF. Note that the squadrons original Donald Duck image has been superimposed over a Type-2 U.S. national emblem. This modification reverted to the original configuration with the introduction of the new Type-3 emblem.

Taken while still assigned to the 8thAAF, this photo clearly shows the insignia of the 307thFS neatly painted on the cockpit access hatch of this U.S. serving Mk.Vb. This application was a common practice within the unit while with the Eighth.

*SQUADRONS OF THE 31ST FG WERE OFTEN ATTACHED TO OTHER AIRFIELDS THROUGHOUT ENGLAND WHILE ASSIGNED TO THE 8THAAF

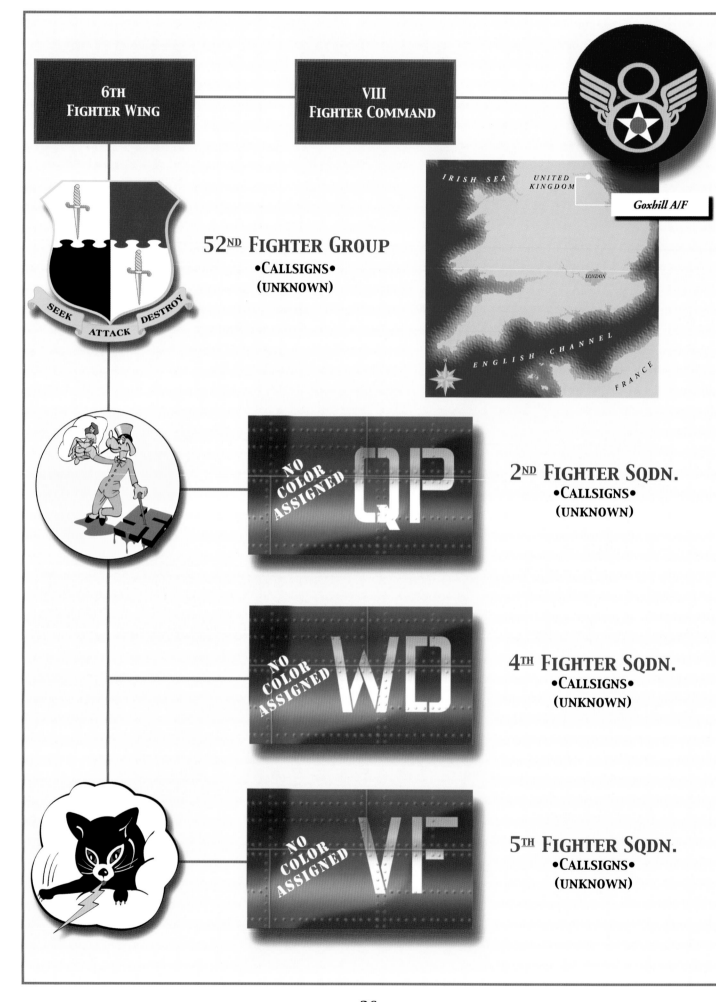

6TH FIGHTER WING

VIII FIGHTER COMMAND

Goxhill A/F

IRISH SEA
UNITED KINGDOM
LONDON
ENGLISH CHANNEL
FRANCE

52ND FIGHTER GROUP
•CALLSIGNS•
(UNKNOWN)

SEEK ATTACK DESTROY

NO COLOR ASSIGNED QP

2ND FIGHTER SQDN.
•CALLSIGNS•
(UNKNOWN)

NO COLOR ASSIGNED WD

4TH FIGHTER SQDN.
•CALLSIGNS•
(UNKNOWN)

NO COLOR ASSIGNED VF

5TH FIGHTER SQDN.
•CALLSIGNS•
(UNKNOWN)

52ND FIGHTER GROUP

'SEEK-ATTACK-DESTROY'

ASSIGNED 8TH AAF/13-JUL-42
STATION NO.345
GOXHILL A/F, LINCOLNSHIRE
C.26-AUG-42 THRU C.1-NOV-42
STATION CALLSIGN:
(UNKNOWN)

CAMPAIGNS
- AIR COMBAT, EAME THEATER •
- AIR OFFENSIVE-EUROPE •
- ALGERIA-FRENCH MOROCCO • TUNISIA •
- SICILY • NAPLES-FOGGIA • ROME-ARNO •
- NORMANDY • NORTHERN FRANCE •
- SOUTHERN FRANCE • NORTH APPINES •
- RHINELAND • CENTRAL EUROPE • PO VALLEY •

A note on squadron insignia. The 2ndFS sometimes incorporated a written slogan within its' insignia design but whether this was common practice or random application is uncertain at this time. Also, the insignia often used today in connection with the 4th FS was not adopted by that unit until several years after the war and the precise wartime combat insignia, if that unit did indeed have one, had not been determined by the time this manuscript was scheduled to be shipped off to the printers. The photo below nicely illustrates the application of the 5thFS insignia to one of the squadrons aircraft. Note that the overall image size is considerably larger and positioned much further forward on the fuselage than the 307thFS insignia on page 35.

All squadrons of the 52nd Fighter Group were initially assigned to Eglinton A/F in Northern Ireland for training purposes. The 5th FtrSqdn would remain at this station until the groups ultimate transfer to the Twelfth Air Force. The 2nd and 4th Fighter Squadrons, however, engaged in numerous sorties along the French coast in conjunction with RAF Fighter Command. These combat operations were conducted from 27Aug thru 11Sep42.

All markings displayed by the 52nd were of identical size, placement and color as those used by both the 4th and 31st FtrSqdns.

As was the case with all American serving Spitfires, the outer yellow ring was omitted from the upper Type-2 US wing roundel.

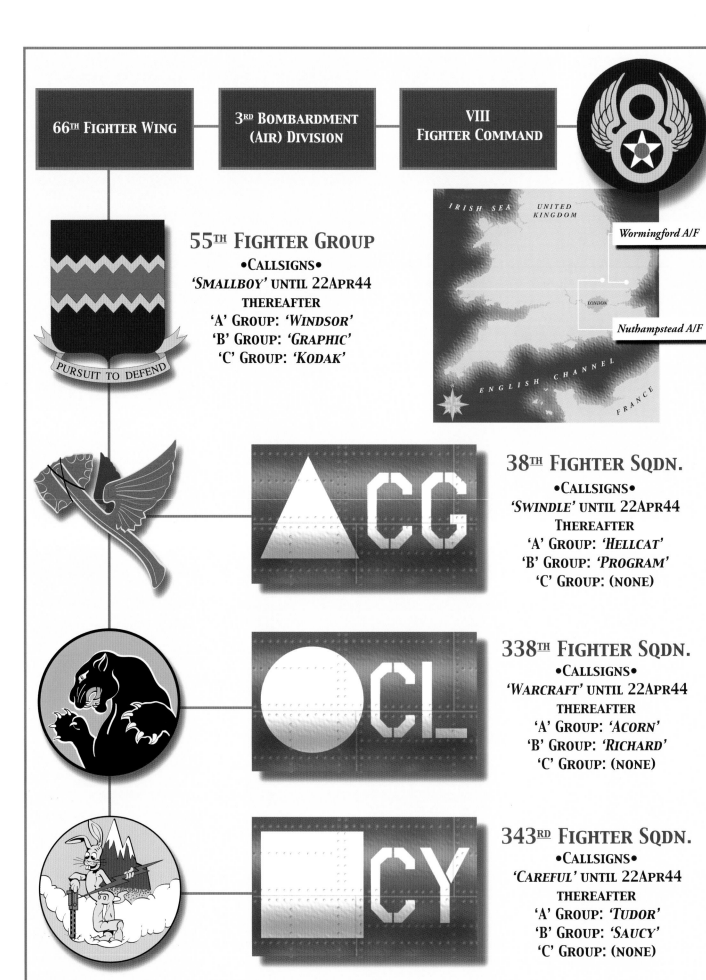

66ᵀᴴ FIGHTER WING — **3ᴿᴰ BOMBARDMENT (AIR) DIVISION** — **VIII FIGHTER COMMAND**

PURSUIT TO DEFEND

55ᵀᴴ FIGHTER GROUP
•CALLSIGNS•
'SMALLBOY' UNTIL 22APR44
THEREAFTER
'A' GROUP: *'WINDSOR'*
'B' GROUP: *'GRAPHIC'*
'C' GROUP: *'KODAK'*

IRISH SEA · UNITED KINGDOM

Wormingford A/F

LONDON

Nuthampstead A/F

ENGLISH CHANNEL · FRANCE

CG

38ᵀᴴ FIGHTER SQDN.
•CALLSIGNS•
'SWINDLE' UNTIL 22APR44
THEREAFTER
'A' GROUP: *'HELLCAT'*
'B' GROUP: *'PROGRAM'*
'C' GROUP: (NONE)

CL

338ᵀᴴ FIGHTER SQDN.
•CALLSIGNS•
'WARCRAFT' UNTIL 22APR44
THEREAFTER
'A' GROUP: *'ACORN'*
'B' GROUP: *'RICHARD'*
'C' GROUP: (NONE)

CY

343ᴿᴰ FIGHTER SQDN.
•CALLSIGNS•
'CAREFUL' UNTIL 22APR44
THEREAFTER
'A' GROUP: *'TUDOR'*
'B' GROUP: *'SAUCY'*
'C' GROUP: (NONE)

55TH FIGHTER GROUP
'PURSUIT TO DEFEND'

ASSIGNED 8TH AAF/12-SEP-43
1.) STATION NO.131
NUTHAMPSTEAD A/F, HERTFORDSHIRE
C.14-SEP-43 THRU 15-APR-44
STATION CALLSIGN: 'ROCKCREEK'
2.) STATION NO.159
WORMINGFORD A/F, ESSEX
C.16-APR-44 THRU 21-JUL-45
STATION CALLSIGN: 'FUSSPOT'

CAMPAIGNS
• AMERICAN THEATER • AIR OFFENSIVE-EUROPE •
• NORMANDY • NORTHERN FRANCE • RHINELAND •
• ARDENNES-ALSACE • CENTRAL EUROPE •

An interesting shot of what appears to be a mission tally panel applied just forward the canopy of this 55th Fighter Group P-51.

Although this image may seen redundant, its purpose here is to illustrate the often considerable chasm between initial design and ultimate application. The image on the facing page represents the original 38thFS insignia as it was submitted to the Air Corps for approval. This image is what more often than not ended up as representing this unit once overseas. Not exactly a match! This is the frustrating, and at the same time fascinating aspect of U.S. combat insignia research.

The 55th Fighter Group began operations with P-38H and later 'J' Series Lightnings and began their transition to the P-51D Mustang in July of 1944. As with other groups which had made a similar conversion, some of the aircraft earlier marking traditions were slowly discarded. In the photo to the immediate right we are afforded a good view of the forward fuselage area of one of the groups original P-38s. Note the mission tally panel, very much the same application as that employed by the 20th Fighter Group when that unit also flew the Lightning. And like the 20th, the use of these type of markings within the 55th Fighter Group dwindled with their transtion to the P-51.

The most interesting feature in the photo at left is what's left of the original D-Day Invasion Stripes. Given the narrow beam of the Mustang fuselage, it causes one to ponder whether or not it might have made more sense to have simply dispensed with these markings altogether. As a recognition factor, they would appear rather useless beyond much more than rock throwing range. This does however serve to again illustrate the wide diversity of tactical marking applications that occurred within 8thAAF units during the war.

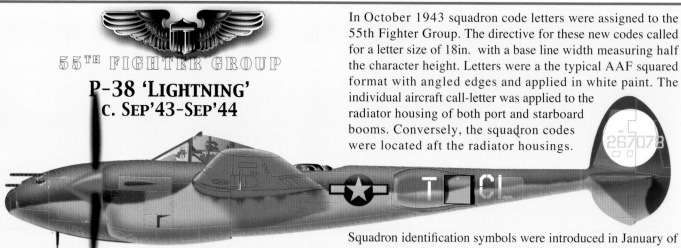

P-38 'LIGHTNING'
C. SEP'43-SEP'44

In October 1943 squadron code letters were assigned to the 55th Fighter Group. The directive for these new codes called for a letter size of 18in. with a base line width measuring half the character height. Letters were a the typical AAF squared format with angled edges and applied in white paint. The individual aircraft call-letter was applied to the radiator housing of both port and starboard booms. Conversely, the squadron codes were located aft the radiator housings.

A considerable number of pilots within the 55th Fighter Group opted to have the white areas of the Type-3 national insignia 'grayed-out' which entailed reapplying a mixture of white and black over the existing white insignia areas. It was felt by some American flyers that the bright white star sandwiched the two horizontal white bars provided enemy pilots and gunners with a convenient 'aiming point' in combat situations. Whether this belief had merit or not is open to debate today, but as the Allies gained aerial supremacy over the skies of Western Europe, this issue diminished in importance and this practice discarded.

Squadron identification symbols were introduced in January of 1944. These were applied in white paint with a specified size of 30in. at the greatest measure to the outward facing surfaces of both tail fins. This procedure obscured the original factory serial numbers and these were not reinstated on a number of the groups aircraft. In other instances these numbers were in fact repainted over the new symbols in either yellow or black.

In March of 1944 the 55th Fighter Group, in an effort to provide their combat aircraft with a greater aerial recognition factor, approved the application of red paint to the engine cowlings of the groups Lightnings. This was not an official 8th AAF unit color designation and lasted only briefly as word had already reached the group of its pending conversion to the P-51 Mustang. Ending almost before it began, this unit marking consisted of a red spinner with an additional red section applied to, and encircling, the forward engine cowling. Some estimates state that this cowling application was supposed to encompass approximately 20in. back from the leading edge of the cowling, other estimates state as much as 40in. of total cowling surface area was to allocated this marking devise.

The 'Droop Snoot' nose (see Introduction) began to appear on 55thFG Lightnings sometime in April 1944. As this particular application to P-38s seem to have proven an effective method for creating confusion among enemy pilots and was soon adopted as a standard application on all 55thFG combat aircraft.

D-Day

With the exception of the squadron tail markers the combat aircraft of the 55th Fighter Group were the quintessential, generic, ETO serving P-38 Lightning. In point of fact, the 20th, 364th and 479th Fighter Squadrons, all flying the P-38 at this same time, utilized these same markings to identify their own respective squadrons. By late Spring these other three groups had begun to employ the use of color markings as a means of improving the unit recognition factor. The 55th Fighter Group however, with the exception of their brief dalliance with the red engine cowlings, never adopted a color scheme while equipped with the P-38 Lightning.

P-51 'MUSTANG'
c. JUL'44-JUN'45

While in transition training with their new Mustangs, the 55th Fighter Group made its first attempt at a group color recognition image. Without seeking higher approval the 55thFG began applying green paint to tail section including the rudder and top horizontal surfaces of a number of assigned aircraft. The paint used was most likely RAF Light Green or something cooked up by the maintenance crews to approximate that particular hue. Tail serial numbers were overpainted with no attempt to reinstate them.

White squadron symbols were applied and the once black QIM's located on the upper surfaces of the stabilizers were all repainted white. Although the same squadron codes from the groups P-38's were transferred to the new Mustangs, no such letter codes are known to have been applied during this period, which was to last just a little under two months.

By the time the 55thFG had become combat operational with their new Mustangs, SHAEF had already proposed the gradual phasing out of these devises. Consequently the 'half-marker' post D-Day pattern was applied to virtually all the groups aircraft.

While some units were very fastidious when it came to filling in the stencil lines on their aircraft, the 55thFG didn't appear to be much concerned with this particuliar detail.

Beginning in July 1944 the groups P-51s began to display the nose pattern depicted above. The same green as was used on the previous tail configuration was again employed for the new nose pattern. Although not unilaterally adopted within the 55thFG, the rather unusual configuration shown on this aircraft was applied to a number of the units Mustangs and made for a distinctive image. This particular 'camouflage' pattern would all but disappear by years end with a final image adaptation.

With the exception of the 38thFS, the other two squadrons comprising the 55thFG adopted recognition colors which began appearing on their respective aircraft by the end of 1944. The 338thFS employed green while the 343rd utilized yellow. The 38th ultimately began to apply red to its rudders but not until about a month and a half before Germanys surrender on May 7th 1945.

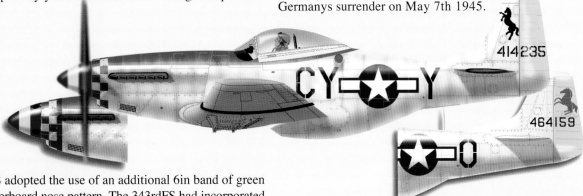

The 338thFS adopted the use of an additional 6in band of green aft the checkerboard nose pattern. The 343rdFS had incorporated the use of a thin red stripe which originally followed the contour of the camouflage paint scheme. Use of this devise was eventually modified to conform to the bottom edge of the antiglare panel. This application was soon expanded upon and, as depicted above, ultimately framed in the antiglare panel and entire canopy structure. This configuration was later adopted as a group identification element and by the end of March 1945, had been applied to all 55th Fighter Group combat Mustangs.

Tail numbers began to appear again on 55thFG aircraft with the adoption of the colored rudders. Another innovation of the 343rdFS, a mustang silhouette began appearing on a number of the squadrons P-51s in late 1944. Although placement and exact configuration varied slightly from one application to another, this symbol nevertheless became a recognizable image of that unit. A few of the Groups aircraft continued to display the black QIM's markings until the cessation of hostilities.

65TH FIGHTER WING	2ND BOMBARDMENT (AIR) DIVISION	VIII FIGHTER COMMAND

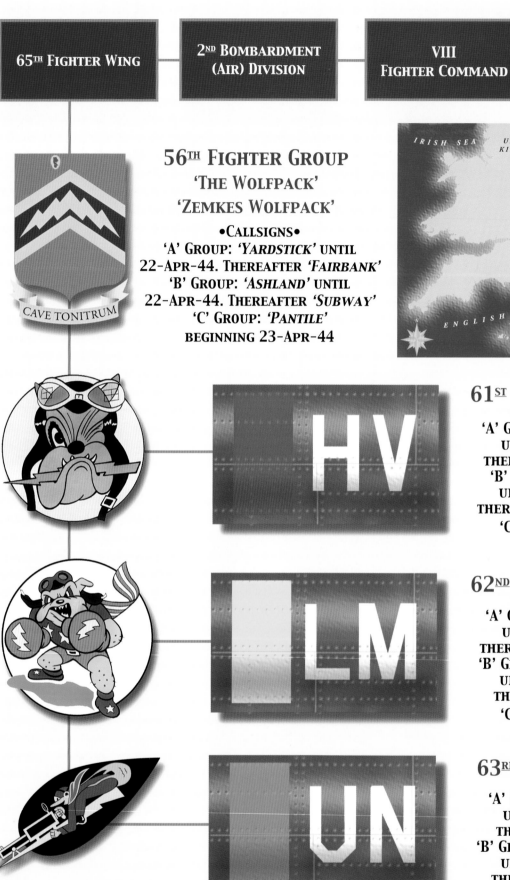

56TH FIGHTER GROUP
'THE WOLFPACK'
'ZEMKES WOLFPACK'
•CALLSIGNS•
'A' GROUP: 'YARDSTICK' UNTIL
22-APR-44. THEREAFTER 'FAIRBANK'
'B' GROUP: 'ASHLAND' UNTIL
22-APR-44. THEREAFTER 'SUBWAY'
'C' GROUP: 'PANTILE'
BEGINNING 23-APR-44

CAVE TONITRUM

IRISH SEA *UNITED KINGDOM*

Horsham St.Faith A/F

LONDON

Boxted A/F

Halesworth A/F

Kingscliffe A/F

ENGLISH CHANNEL

FRANCE

HV

61ST FIGHTER SQDN.
•CALLSIGNS•
'A' GROUP: 'KEYWORTH'
UNTIL22-APR-44,
THEREAFTER 'WHIPPET'
'B' GROUP: 'HALSTED'
UNTIL 22-APR-44,
THEREAFTER 'HOUSEHOLD'
'C' GROUP: (NONE)

LM

62ND FIGHTER SQDN.
•CALLSIGNS•
'A' GROUP: 'WOODFIRE'
UNTIL22-APR-44,
THEREAFTER 'PLATFORM'
'B' GROUP: 'GROUNDHOG'
UNTIL 22-APR-44,
THEREAFTER 'ICEJUG'
'C' GROUP: (NONE)

UN

63RD FIGHTER SQDN.
•CALLSIGNS•
'A' GROUP: 'POSTGATE'
UNTIL22-APR-44,
THEREAFTER 'DAILY'
'B' GROUP: 'NORTHGROVE'
UNTIL 22-APR-44,
THEREAFTER 'YORKER'
'C' GROUP: (NONE)

56TH FIGHTER GROUP

'BEWARE THE THUNDERBOLT'

ASSIGNED 8TH AAF/12-JAN-43
*STATION No.365
HALESWORTH A/F, SUFFOLK
8-JUL-43 THRU 18-APR-44
STATION CALLSIGN:
'STURDY'

CAMPAIGNS
• AMERICAN THEATER • AIR OFFENSIVE-EUROPE •
• NORMANDY • NORTHERN FRANCE • RHINELAND •
• ARDENNES-ALSACE • CENTRAL EUROPE •

* The 56th FG was actually stationed at four different air fields during the course of the war, five if you care to include a post war assignment to Little Walden A/F from September 9th thru October 10th 1945. The first two war time stations were at Kings Cliffe A/F in Northhamptonshire (Station No.367) from 13Jan-5Apr, 1943. Next came Horsham St. Faith located in Norfolk (Station No.123) after which came Halesworth A/F which was followed by a posting to Boxted A/F, in Essex (Station No.150/call-sign 'Dogday') from 18Apr44 until 9Sep45.

Shortly after arriving in England the 56thFG began identifying its aircraft with a *plane-in-group* method system. From the middle of February thru the end of March 1943 the following numerical sequences were directed to be applied in white paint on both sides of the fuselage, just forward the intercooler doors;

Headquarters / 01-09
61st FtrSqdn / 10-39
62nd FtrSqdn / 240-269
63rd FtrSqdn / 370-399

The paint would hardly have been dry on these numbers when they were ordered replaced with newly issued squadron codes.

The photo below of the battle damaged tail section of a 56thFG aircraft shows the *hinge centered* positioning of the 7 1/2 in tall production number typical on late model P-47D-RE and all RA production series Thunderbolts. Of special interest here are the *squared* inter-surface corner areas of the numerals themselves. By comparison, this particular style of stenciling is a departure from the familiar *angled* inter-corner edges more commonly associated with U.S./E.T.O. combat aircraft during this period.

Another battle damaged Thunderbolt, this one belonging to the 61st Fighter Squadron. Even at this early stage (as evidenced by the style of national insignia), the 56th Fighter Group had begun to express its individuality in regards to unit identity. Note the interesting application of the fuselage call-letter and squadron code. In most cases unpainted stencil lines were the result of haste or indifference, neither of which is the case in this example. Although the original stencil lines remain visible, they have been carefully filled in with the same paint used to outline the letters. Close examination of the aircraft tail number shows that the numerals have been reapplied with the same style stencil, albeit smaller size, as those used on the fuselage codes.

REPBULIC P-47 'THUNDERBOLT'
C. FEB'42-SEP'45

Inasmuch as style is concerned, the 56th Fighter Group may well be referred to as the Beau Brummell of the Eighth Air Force. From the Groups earliest stages of deployment in England this unit began to establish a unique visual identity that would unmistakably distinguish itself, and its individual squadrons. In the latter part of February 1943, the Groups squadrons received their new fuselage codes and, with the exception of individual markings, spent the remainder of the year looking pretty much like the illustration below depicts. The only real change came with the introduction of the 'star &bars' national insignia which necessitated repositioning the call-letter.

Beginning in March/April 1944 all three squadrons comprising the 56thFG began experimenting with a wide variety of paint schemes for their aircraft. These ran the gambit from a full coverage of 'dark' green, most likely an RAF Light Green, some of which received an additional application of Ocean Grey in patterns varying from a more traditional 'stripping' to a 'blotching' motif. The photo above depicts the former style.

In the opening weeks of 1944 things began to change very quickly for the 56thFG, identity wise. The Group applied for and was subsequently granted permission to adopt the application of colors to its aircraft as a better means of aircraft recognition. Red, yellow and blue (light) paint were selected for the 61st, 62nd and 63rd Fighter Squadrons respectively. These colors were to replace the existing white QIMs on the engine cowlings. Some at VIII FC must have thought this a pretty good idea for the paint on 56thFG aircraft hadn't quite dried when a directive was issued assigning each fighter group within the Eighth AF its own specific recognition color, which in the case of the 56thFG turned out to be red. The Group HQ opted to adopt the same bright shade of red only recently put to use by the 61stFS. This may very well have been a conscious effort on the part of the Groups brass to reduce the repainting of its aircraft by one-third.

63RD FIGHTER SQUADRON

62ND FIGHTER SQUADRON

61ST FIGHTER SQUADRON

When in March the 56th Fighter Group was assigned red as its official unit recognition color, the group recieved permission from VIII FC to continue the use of its designated squadron colors re-located to the aircrafts rudders. Someone within the 56th FG command was apparently ahead of the game in recognizing the importance of individual aircraft unit recognition.

For reasons uncertain today the 63rd Fighter Squadron initially opted not to apply their light blue color to its aircraft. However, the following September of '44, the powers that be at 63rd HQ reversed their initial decision and ordered its ground crews to paint all squadron combat aircraft rudders in the original light blue it had previously displayed on its ships engine cowlings.

C. JAN-APR'45

The 61st Fighter Squadron had perhaps the widest assortment of paint schemes applied to their ships during most of 1944. By the beginning of 1945 however all three squadrons settled on their own distinctive patterns for their respective aircraft. In the case of the 61stFS, a bluish-black paint was selected as that units dominant color. This particular shade of black does not match any existing hue within either British or American paint inventories. After reviewing available color photographs of the period, a best guess would be that this was most probably a 'home-brew' of an ANA Insignia Blue and Black with possibly a touch of Insignia White thrown in as an light tinting agent.

As evidenced in this relatively early photo in the Groups history, the squadrons of the 56thFG payed little attention to the matter of filling in stencil lines on their aircraft. This was true of both tail and fuselage applications and was in fact a feature that was to become almost a secondary signature element of this unit. While not all stencil lines were to remain unfilled on 56thFG aircraft, it was nevertheless a prominent feature, and common on many of the Groups P-47's.

A white vertical stripe was often painted along the inner tail fin surface parallel to and just forward of the rudder. The aircraft tail number was reapplied in squadron red as were the fuselage codes which were additionally outlined with Insignia White to enhance legibility. The contour edges of the national insignia tended to disappear almost completely when set against this particular paint. The problem was solved by outlining the insignia with a lighter shade of blue paint, reminiscent of the earlier red outline displayed on U.S. aircraft prior to June 1943. Typically the under-surfaces of aircraft receiving this treatment remained in the original natural metal finish.

By January 1945 the 56thFG had received a substantial number of 'M' Series P-47's. Although these aircraft were delivered to the Group in a natural metal finish, many would become adorned with a 61st Squadron 'signature' paint job and retain same until wars end.

62ND FIGHTER SQUADRON
56TH FIGHTER GROUP
c. Jan-Apr'45

The 62nd Fighter Squadron opted to adopt a more traditional disruptive paint scheme for many of its fighters which consisted of two RAF colors; Ocean Grey applied over a base coat of Dark Green. While not all aircraft within the 62nd were to receive this treatment, enough did to qualify this particular application as a signature piece for the squadron. In addition to the typical 'stripped' effect, there was a 'blotching, technique which was also utilized, both of which are depicted below. A third paint theme of the 62ndFG consisted of an overall application of Dark Green with no secondary color applied. An additional variation was a solid top-side application of Dark Green over a standard lower fuselage/wing coat of Neutral Grey.

As evidenced by this photograph, not all Thunderbolts assigned to the 62nd Fighter Squadron bore a two-color paint scheme. This particular photo was taken sometime between September and December of 1944 judging from the post D-Day Stripes.

Immediately following the standardization by VIII Fighter Command of fighter group color designations within the European Theater of Operations in March 1944, and the subsequent assigning of a red engine cowling as the official 56th Fighter Group color designator, the 62ndFS began to paint the rudders of their aircraft as well as the fuselage codes and tail numbers with ANA Identification Yellow. The 62nd FS additionally employed their own rather unique style of fuselage letter stencils which unto themselves became somewhat of a recognition element.

Another feature characteristic of 56th Fighter Group paint schemes was the habit of leaving the leading edges of both the wings and horizontal stabilizers unpainted. The exact intention of this procedure is uncertain today, however it has been suggested that it had to do more with a maintenance issue than one of esthetics. The leading wing edges of any combat aircraft are subjected to a high degree of stress and friction, thus requiring constant attention once painted.

63ʳᵈ FIGHTER SQUADRON
56ᵗʰ FIGHTER GROUP
c. Jan–Apr '45

The 63rdFS developed arguably one of the most striking 'camouflage' paint schemes to be displayed on 8thAAF fighters. This effect was created combining two RAF colors, Azure Blue applied over Mediterranean Blue, in a disruptive pattern. While the concealment aspect of this particular color combination might come into question under the prevailing circumstances, it nevertheless made a definitive statement insofar as unit identification was concerned, and this was undoubtedly the primary, if not sole intention of this design.

This wheels-up landing shot provides an excellent view of an early 63rd Fighter Squadron Thunderbolt. This appears to be one of those ships that received an overall application of RAF Dark Green sometime in the spring/summer of 1943. Note the red outlined national insignia and white UK nose/tail markings.

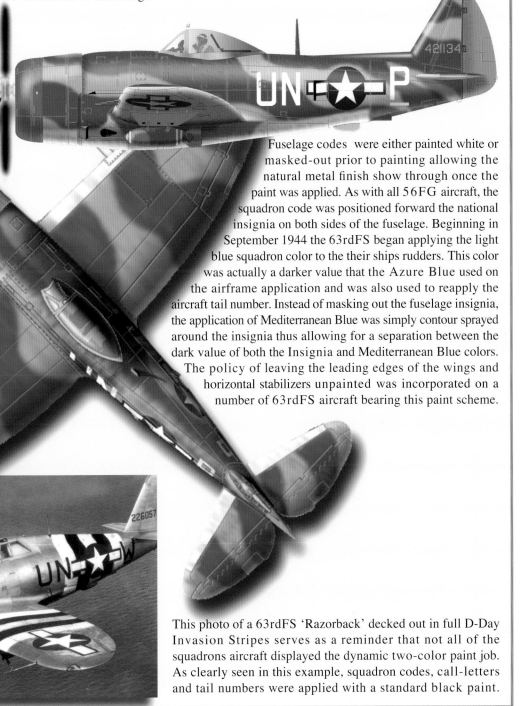

Fuselage codes were either painted white or masked-out prior to painting allowing the natural metal finish show through once the paint was applied. As with all 56FG aircraft, the squadron code was positioned forward the national insignia on both sides of the fuselage. Beginning in September 1944 the 63rdFS began applying the light blue squadron color to the their ships rudders. This color was actually a darker value that the Azure Blue used on the airframe application and was also used to reapply the aircraft tail number. Instead of masking out the fuselage insignia, the application of Mediterranean Blue was simply contour sprayed around the insignia thus allowing for a separation between the dark value of both the Insignia and Mediterranean Blue colors. The policy of leaving the leading edges of the wings and horizontal stabilizers unpainted was incorporated on a number of 63rdFS aircraft bearing this paint scheme.

This photo of a 63rdFS 'Razorback' decked out in full D-Day Invasion Stripes serves as a reminder that not all of the squadrons aircraft displayed the dynamic two-color paint job. As clearly seen in this example, squadron codes, call-letters and tail numbers were applied with a standard black paint.

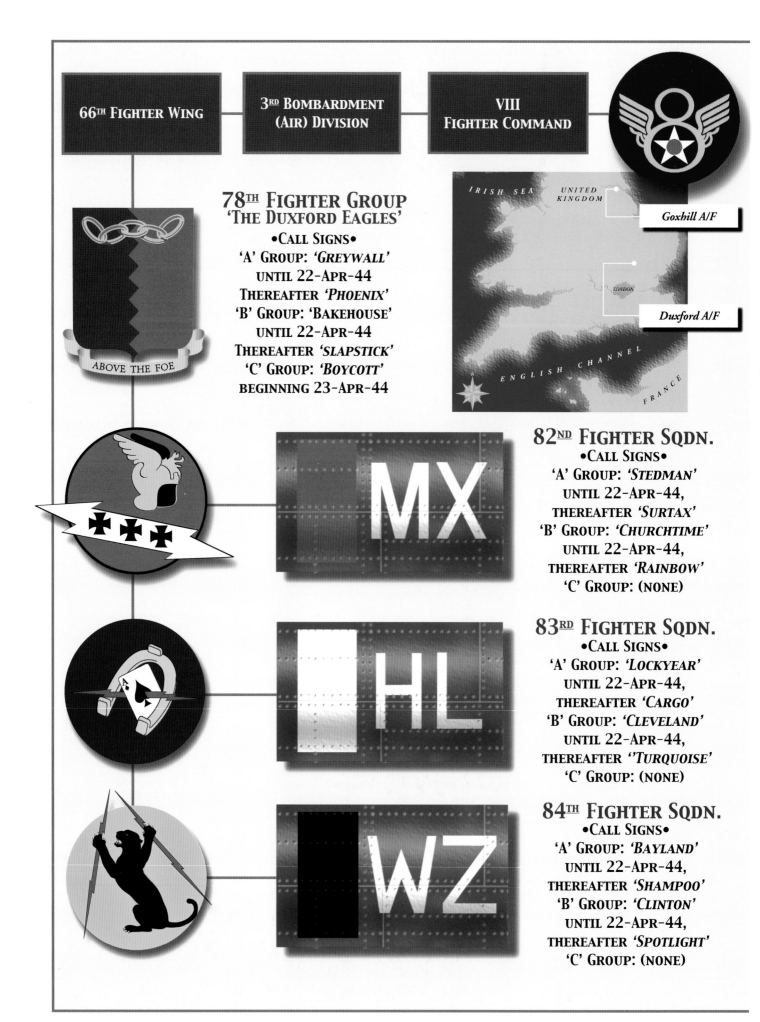

66ᵀᴴ Fighter Wing — **3ᴿᴰ Bombardment (Air) Division** — **VIII Fighter Command**

78ᵀᴴ Fighter Group
'The Duxford Eagles'
•Call Signs•
'A' Group: *'Greywall'*
until 22-Apr-44
Thereafter *'Phoenix'*
'B' Group: 'Bakehouse'
until 22-Apr-44
Thereafter *'Slapstick'*
'C' Group: *'Boycott'*
beginning 23-Apr-44

ABOVE THE FOE

Goxhill A/F

IRISH SEA — UNITED KINGDOM

LONDON

Duxford A/F

ENGLISH CHANNEL — FRANCE

82ᴺᴰ Fighter Sqdn.
•Call Signs•
'A' Group: *'Stedman'*
until 22-Apr-44,
thereafter *'Surtax'*
'B' Group: *'Churchtime'*
until 22-Apr-44,
thereafter *'Rainbow'*
'C' Group: (none)

MX

83ᴿᴰ Fighter Sqdn.
•Call Signs•
'A' Group: *'Lockyear'*
until 22-Apr-44,
thereafter *'Cargo'*
'B' Group: *'Cleveland'*
until 22-Apr-44,
thereafter *''Turquoise'*
'C' Group: (none)

HL

84ᵀᴴ Fighter Sqdn.
•Call Signs•
'A' Group: *'Bayland'*
until 22-Apr-44,
thereafter *'Shampoo'*
'B' Group: *'Clinton'*
until 22-Apr-44,
thereafter *'Spotlight'*
'C' Group: (none)

WZ

78TH FIGHTER GROUP
'ABOVE THE FOE'

ASSIGNED 8TH AAF/C.NOV-'43
1.) STATION NO. 345
GOXHILL A/F, LINCOLNSWHIRE
C.DEC-43 THRU C.APR-'43
STATION CALL SIGN: (UNKNOWN)
2.) STATION NO.357
DUXFORD A/F, CAMBRIDGESHIRE
C.3-APR-43 THRU C.10-OCT-45
STATION CALL SIGN: 'RUTLEY'

CAMPAIGNS
• AIR OFFENSIVE-EUROPE •
• NORMANDY • NORTHERN FRANCE • RHINELAND •
• ARDENNES-ALSACE • CENTRAL EUROPE •

LOCKHEED P-38 'LIGHTNING'
C. DEC-'42

One of the first units trained and equipped with the P-38G, the 78thFG departed New York harbor for England on 24Nov42. Upon arrival the 78th was originally assigned to Goxhill A/F on 1Dec42 where they underwent additional training until 3Apr43 when they were transferred to their permanent base at Duxford A/F. However in February 1943, just prior to this transfer, most of the Groups pilots and Lightnings were reassigned to the 12thAAF for combat duty in North Africa. In the interim the 78th was re-equipped and retrained with P-47 Thunderbolts with which the unit would commence combat operations.

During their initial deployment in Great Britain the 78thFG adopted an aircraft identification system similar to that utilized when training in the United States. This entailed the stenciling of an *aircraft-in-group* number on both outside facing engine cowlings as well as both radiator housings. The groups P-38s bore the Type-3 USAAF National Insignia when first deployed to England however these were soon modified with the application of the now familiar 2inch UK *friendly forces* yellow surround. Additionally, both propeller spinners of each aircraft were painted in their respective assigned squadron color.

The *plane-in-group* method of aircraft identification utilizes by the 78th involved the application of specified numbers in same respective squadron colors as those used on the ships propeller spinners. The numbers assigned are depicted in the graphic to the immediate left. As previously mentioned, these were stenciled onto both the radiator housing and engine cowlings in characters approximately 18 inches in height. In most cases the stencil lines remained in their original un-painted state.

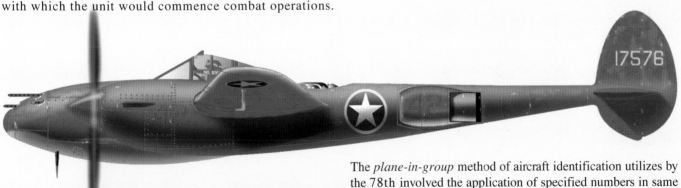

HEADQUARTERS	01-09
82ND FTR SQDN	10-39
84TH FTR SQDN	70-99

REPBULIC P-47 'THUNDERBOLT'
C. FEB'42-JAN'45

At the urging of the British Air Ministry, the white UK recognition stripes and yellow cocarde surround were applied to all 78thFG P-47C's shortly after arrival . It was widely feared that allied antiaircraft gun crews would too easily mistake the airborne Thunderbolt silhouette with the German FW190, thus greatly increasing the risk of friendly fire incidents.

The Thunderbolts, which replaced the 78thFGs Lightnings, were initially identified with the same *plane-in-group* numbering system as those originally utilized on the P-38s. The adjacent photo shows the remnants of such numbers just prior to being repainted with new code letters. This *plane-in-group* system was replaced with white 24in tall squadron code letter combinations in March 1943 and would ultimately be applied to the Groups P-51 Mustangs.

The 'checkerboard' cowling marking began to appear on the Groups P-47s at the same time the new squadron codes were adopted (Mar'43). The *squares* were in fact 8"x7" *rectangles* applied six *squares* per row

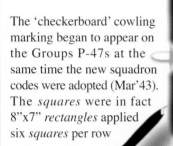

Unpainted P-47s began arriving at the 78thFG in April 1944 and in accordance with a VIII Fighter Command directive, painted the upper surfaces of these aircraft with a RAF Dark Green and a Sky Blue application applied to most under-surfaces. Tail numbers were reapplied with 7in-8in tall yellow numerals. This was in anticipation of the Groups potential post D-Day deployment within Continental Europe and the 78thFG would continue to adhere to this camouflage policy until the end of 1944. Natural metal finished P-47s did participate in Group combat operations during this time frame but only until time allowed for the application of the aforementioned paint scheme. When D-Day Invasion Stripes were applied, the fuselage codes were masked-out prior to the painting process and not obscured in any way. Squadron colors did not begin appearing on the Groups tail rudders until late October of '44. The existing UK Marker on the tails was sometimes removed with this new application, in other instances these devises were simply over-painted.

In late 1943, the 78FG squadrons inventory began to exceed the previous allotment of twenty-six. Aircraft falling into this 'overflow' category were so designated with the addition of a *bar,* which was located just below the fuselage call letter.

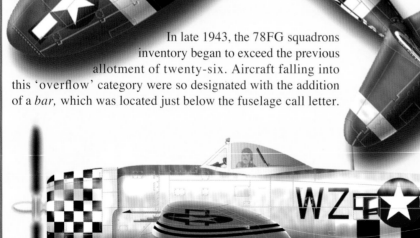

78TH FIGHTER GROUP

NORTH AMERICAN P-51 'MUSTANG'
C. DEC'44-AUG'45

Tail rudders received squadron color almost immediately after the new P-51's arrived at the 78thFG maintenance areas. The 83rd Fighter Squadron quickly opted for an additional 2in. contour outline for added visibility. The original tail numbers were simply masked-over prior to rudder paint application leaving an unpainted horizontal strip on the rudder. This policy was soon modified with the numbers being removed entirely and repainted. In the case of the 82nd and 84thFS's, these were relocated entirely forward of the rudder.

78th Fighter Group spinners were equally divided into black & white halves. In flight these created an almost strobe-like effect, creating an illusionary slow motion visual effect.

Squadron codes remained the same size and configuration as those previously used on the Groups P-47s with stencil lines invariably being filled-in. The 82nd and 83rd FSs often accented their fuselage codes with a thin Insignia Red contour outline.

The original 78thFG nose marking consisted of a series of 12"x 12" black squares upon a white background. The size of the squares was quickly modified down to an 8"x 8" motif. The stencils for this configuration were barely cut when the nose pattern was further modified to employ 6"x 6" black squares and this is what was ultimately adopted. The design for the Groups P-51's consisted of a checkerboard scheme similar to that used on the units Thunderbolts. Beginning at the top with equal rows of eight alternating b&w squares, these swept back in a downward arch intersecting at the base of the wing root. Between the wing root and spinner there were a total of twelve such alternating b&w squares. A two inch red border was eventually added to the trailing edge of this pattern to enhance the separation between the white of the pattern and the ships natural metal finish. The Commanding Officer of the 78thFG began a practice which was ultimately adopted by several other Mustangs within the Group. This entailed a pattern of between seven and nine alternating vertical b&w stripes running along both wing tips. A variation on this theme was the application to the same area of respective squadron colors.

In the closing two months of the war the 84th Fighter Squadron adopted the practice of painting the main canopy frame of their Mustangs Insignia Red. This was the favored location of many 78thFG pilots for the application of their individual kill marks.

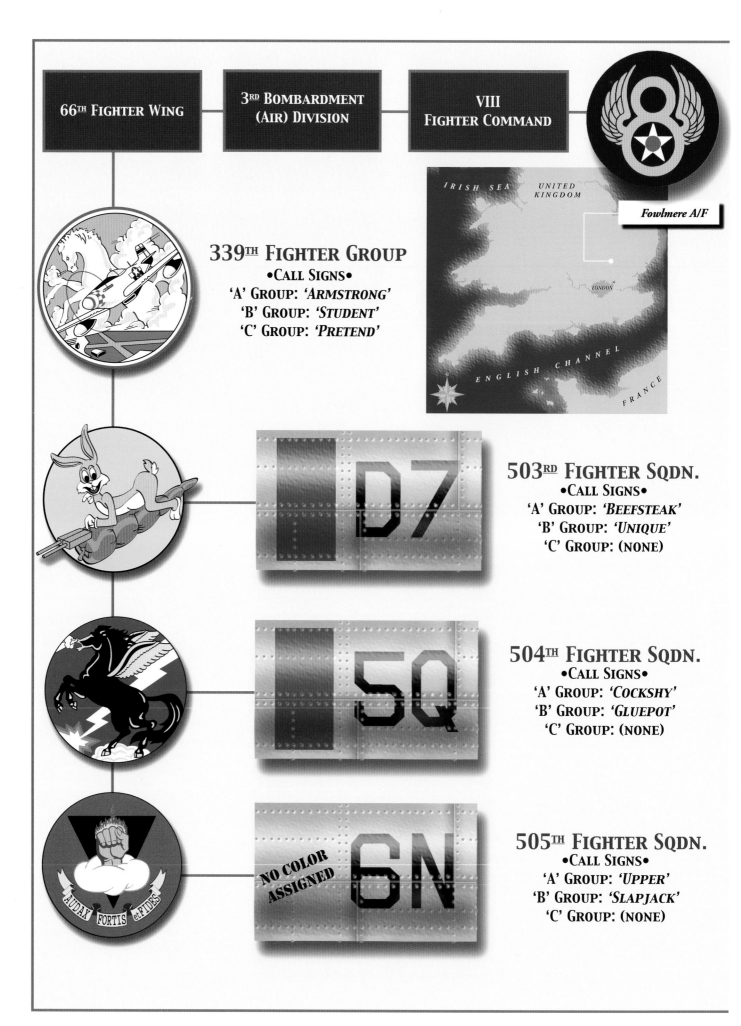

66TH FIGHTER WING — **3RD BOMBARDMENT (AIR) DIVISION** — **VIII FIGHTER COMMAND**

IRISH SEA — *UNITED KINGDOM*

Fowlmere A/F

LONDON

ENGLISH CHANNEL

FRANCE

339TH FIGHTER GROUP
•CALL SIGNS•
'A' GROUP: *'ARMSTRONG'*
'B' GROUP: *'STUDENT'*
'C' GROUP: *'PRETEND'*

503RD FIGHTER SQDN.
•CALL SIGNS•
'A' GROUP: *'BEEFSTEAK'*
'B' GROUP: *'UNIQUE'*
'C' GROUP: (NONE)

D7

504TH FIGHTER SQDN.
•CALL SIGNS•
'A' GROUP: *'COCKSHY'*
'B' GROUP: *'GLUEPOT'*
'C' GROUP: (NONE)

5Q

505TH FIGHTER SQDN.
•CALL SIGNS•
'A' GROUP: *'UPPER'*
'B' GROUP: *'SLAPJACK'*
'C' GROUP: (NONE)

NO COLOR ASSIGNED

6N

AUDAX FORTIS et FIDES

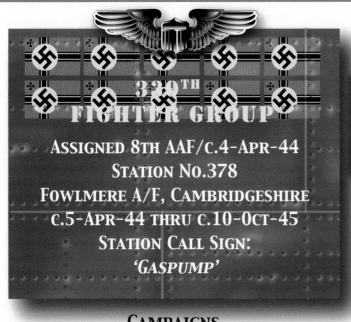

339TH FIGHTER GROUP

ASSIGNED 8TH AAF/C.4-APR-44
STATION NO.378
FOWLMERE A/F, CAMBRIDGESHIRE
C.5-APR-44 THRU C.10-OCT-45
STATION CALL SIGN:
'GASPUMP'

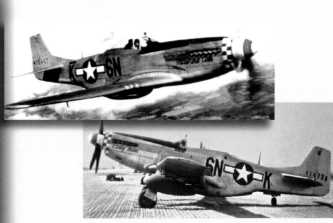

CAMPAIGNS
- **AMERICAN THEATER • AIR OFFENSIVE-EUROPE •**
- **NORMANDY • NORTHERN FRANCE • RHINELAND •**
- **ARDENNES-ALSACE • CENTRAL EUROPE •**

When squadron aircraft inventories increased to numbers exceeding twenty-six, the application of a bar symbol to the call letter was used to denote a 'second-in-series' status. Close examination of the two photos above discloses the bar positioned above the call-letter in the top image clearly indicating that this aircraft was a more recent arrival to the 505thFS. It should be noted that while the bar symbol located above the call letter was the prevalent location within the 339thFtrGrp there were instances where this device was placed *below* the call-letter.

As was the case with most field applied aviation graphics during World War II, subtle variations seem to have been commonplace. Close examination of these three photographs supports this contention. In the top example the aft section of the red & white 'checkerboard' terminates at a point just a bit forward the exhaust manifold cutout while the other two photos show the graphics overlapping the cutout area. Note also the variation in the positioning of the checkered pattern in relationship to this same exhaust cutout. Additionally, some of the *squares* have a decidedly rectangular appearance about them.

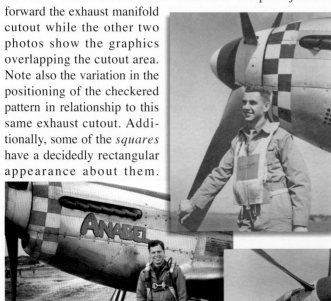

Of particular interest in the above photograph is the graphic image located just aft the call-letter. The aircraft is a P-51B, serial no. 42-006735 assigned to the 505th Fighter Squadron. The bird in flight superimposed over the crescent moon was the symbol denoting 'C ' Flight of the 505thFtrSqdn/339thFtrGrp. Just how wide spread the use of such symbols was among the squadrons of the 339thFG is uncertain at this time but is most certainly a subject worthy of more intense study in the future.

NORTH AMERICAN P-51 'MUSTANG'
C. JUN'44

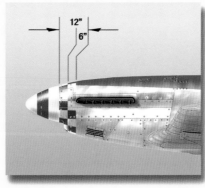

The 339thFG became fully operational with all combat aircraft decorated with the standard black UK/QIMs in addition to their own distinctive unit nose markings. The latter called for an application of Insignia Red over an Identification White base in a configuration very similar to that depicted in the adjacent graphics. As discussed on the previous page however, actual applications within the Group's three squadrons displayed subtle design variations from one aircraft to another. Painting the spinner did not pose much of a problem as this simply entailed dividing the surface area into three equal parts.

Squadron codes were assigned to the 339th Fighter Group immediately upon the unit's arrival in the United Kingdom. Due to the relatively late arrival of the 339th to the ETO, all aircraft assigned to the Groups squadrons were P-51Bs of the natural metal finish variety and thus displayed their respective codes exclusively in black paint. These complied with VIII Fighter Commands prescribed size, letter style and placement for similarly equipped Mustang units. Later replacement aircraft would include the 'C', 'D' and 'K' Series P-51s. No individual squadron colors were assigned to the 339th Fighter Group the latter part of 1944. As with other British based USAAF units, full D-Day Invasion Stripes were applied to all of the Groups serviceable combat aircraft immediately prior to the Normandy Invasion and would continue to be displayed by all squadrons of the 339thFG until directed to convert to the 'half stripe' pattern later in the summer of 1944. The aerial photograph at the bottom of this page shows a flight of four 503rdFS Mustangs displaying the typical post D-Day Invasion Stripe pattern on the fuselages. An interesting feature of this photo is that the underwing surfaces of all aircraft carry the single pre invasion black UK/QIM wing markers as opposed to the normal D-Day pattern.

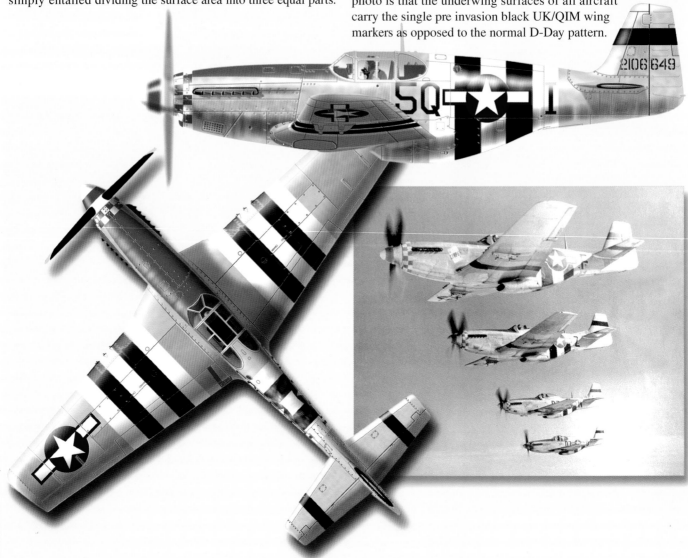

NORTH AMERICAN P-51 'MUSTANG'
c. DEC'44–AUG'45

Individual colors were adopted by the 503rd and 504th Fighter Squadrons in November of 1944 and by early December most of their Mustangs rudders displayed respective unit colors. The 505thFS opted not to adopt a color for some reason and their rudders would remain unpainted for the remainder of the war. The majority of P-51s assigned to the 339thFG did not apply paint to the aircrafts canopy section. There were those few examples however where the Olive Drab antiglare paint used on the upper engine cowling was carried back to encompass the entire main canopy frame as evidenced in the photo below.

In addition to the impressive and well applied 'kill' markings in this photo is the red drop-shadow incorporated as part of this aircrafts squadron code. It should be pointed out that this was the personal mount of the 339th Fighter Groups Commanding Officer, Lt.Col. William C. Clark (circa Apr45), and as such is not to be considered as representational of all 339thFG aircraft.

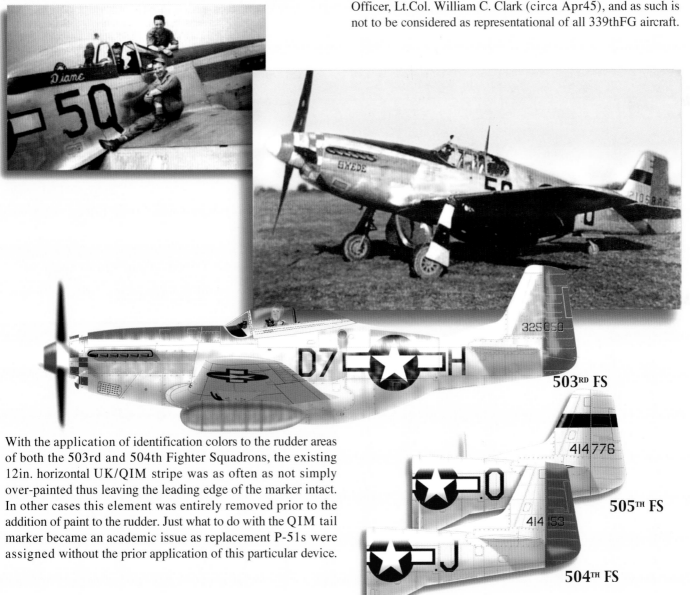

503ᴿᴰ FS

505ᵀᴴ FS

504ᵀᴴ FS

With the application of identification colors to the rudder areas of both the 503rd and 504th Fighter Squadrons, the existing 12in. horizontal UK/QIM stripe was as often as not simply over-painted thus leaving the leading edge of the marker intact. In other cases this element was entirely removed prior to the addition of paint to the rudder. Just what to do with the QIM tail marker became an academic issue as replacement P-51s were assigned without the prior application of this particular device.

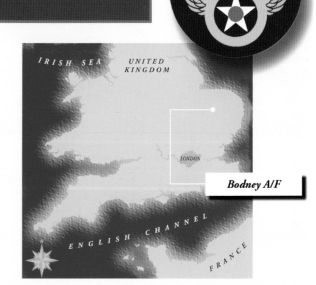

67TH FIGHTER WING	1ST BOMBARDMENT (AIR) DIVISION	VIII FIGHTER COMMAND

352ND FIGHTER GROUP
'THE BLUENOSED BASTARDS OF BODNEY'

•CALL SIGNS•
'HATFIELD' UNTIL 22-APR-44,
THEREAFTER
'A' GROUP: *'TOPSY'*, THAN
'PACKLOAD' FROM APRIL'45
'B' GROUP: *'BEARSKIN'*
'C' GROUP: *'CLOISTER'*

Bodney A/F

328TH FIGHTER SQDN.
•CALL SIGNS•
'TURNDOWN' UNTIL 22-APR-44,
THEREAFTER
'A' GROUP: *'DITTO'*, THAN
'SCREWCAP' FROM APRIL'45
'B' GROUP: *'TARMAC'*
'C' GROUP: (NONE)

486TH FIGHTER SQDN.
•CALL SIGNS•
'HANDSPUN' UNTIL 22-APR-44,
THEREAFTER
'A' GROUP: *'ANGUS'*
'B' GROUP: *'ROCKET'*
'C' GROUP: (NONE)

487TH FIGHTER SQDN.
•CALL SIGNS•
'CROWNPRINCE' UNTIL 22-APR-45,
THEREAFTER
'A' GROUP: *'TRANSPORT'*
'B' GROUP: *'VICAR'*
'C' GROUP: (NONE)

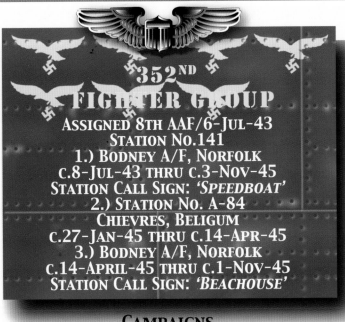

352ND FIGHTER GROUP

ASSIGNED 8TH AAF/6-JUL-43
STATION NO.141
1.) BODNEY A/F, NORFOLK
C.8-JUL-43 THRU C.3-NOV-45
STATION CALL SIGN: 'SPEEDBOAT'
2.) STATION NO. A-84
CHIEVRES, BELIGUM
C.27-JAN-45 THRU C.14-APR-45
3.) BODNEY A/F, NORFOLK
C.14-APRIL-45 THRU C.1-NOV-45
STATION CALL SIGN: 'BEACHOUSE'

CAMPAIGNS

• AIR OFFENSIVE-EUROPE • NORMANDY •
• NORTHERN FRANCE • RHINELAND •
• ARDENNES-ALSACE • CENTRAL EUROPE •

An interesting aspect of 352nd Fighter Group history is the fact that the unit did not adopt a combat insignia until long after the end of World War II, in 1954 to be exact. While this was not by any means a unique situation among USAAF units during the war, it is nevertheless surprising given the importance placed upon such imagery by some of the 352nd's squadron leaders. It is interesting that some commanders simply do not grasp the importance that imagery can play in a unit's *esprit de corps*, whether it's a sports team or military organization. Leaders, both past and present, too often lack the intuitive sense to recognize the correlation between a strong visual identity and good morale. To some this particular aspect of team identity is superfluous, a trite issue fully unworthy of their august attention. Ironically it is the unit that puts forth the effort to project a distinctive visual image that ultimately succeeds in capturing the publics imagination, instills a sense of pride among its members and subsequently ends up leaving an indelible image in the annals of history.

An example of just how attached some individuals can become to an image can be found in the history of the 486th Fighter Squadron. This unit traces its origins to the 21st Pursuit Squadron but was redesignated and reorganized as the 486thFS in 1942 and subsequently adopted the replacement insignia depicted on the preceding page. Many of the existing squadron pilots were so attached to the original insignia that they would continue to display this image on their personal clothing throughout the war.

One officer who was apparently cognizant of the importance of team imagery was than Lt.Col. John C. Meyer, commanding the 487thFS. 'Petie' as the squadrons icon was named was omnipresent in virtually every aspect of squadron life as these photos attest. Today this image has become one of the more familiar combat insignia associated with the 8th AAF in WWII. It may not hurt to mention that as far as unit moral was concerned, the 487thFS under Col.Meyer's command was the only individual squadron within the 8thAAF to be awarded a Distinguished Unit Citation during the course of the war, all other such honors going to units of Group level or higher.

REPUBLIC P-47 'THUNDERBOLT'
C. JUL'43-APR'44

The 352ndFG were assigned individual squadron code letters almost immediately after their arrival in Great Britain. Note the dark blue contour outline on the fuselage insignia. It was a common practice among many units to simply over-paint the existing red outline of Type-3 National Insignia when the replacement Type-4 pattern was subsequently adopted.

Shortly after becoming operational, the combat insignia of the 487th Fighter Squadron began to appear on the forward fuselage area and engine cowlings of several of the units Thunderbolts. Perhaps because of security concerns at that particular time, further application of this image to the squadrons combat aircraft was prohibited and all existing insignia, such as the one above, were ordered removed.

Very early on the 486th Fighter Group began to express a somewhat independent nature. This is reflected in the identification stencils utilized by that squadron to apply codes to its aircraft. The characters have a distinctive rounded appearance to them as opposed to the standard angle-cut edges utilized by its sister squadrons.

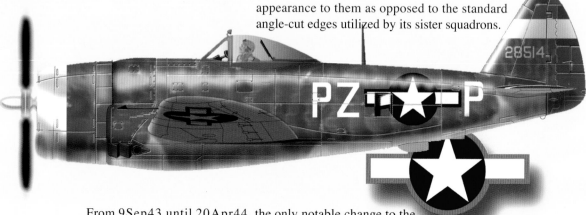

From 9Sep43 until 20Apr44, the only notable change to the markings on 352nd Fighter Group Thunderbolts was the transition from a red outlined Type-3 USAAF National Insignia to the final two color Type-4 pattern. The directive concerning this final modification came within just eleven days (17Sep43) of the Groups commencing actual combat operations.

NORTH AMERICAN P-51 'MUSTANG'
c. MAR'44 / VE-DAY

In March of 1944 the 486th Fighter Squadron began receiving its allocation of 'B' and 'C' Series P-51's, all in a two-color camouflage paint scheme. The following month the 328th and 487th Fighter Squadrons began receiving their replacement Mustangs, all in a natural metal finish. For a very brief period the 352ndFG attempted to identify its new aircraft by replacing the white QIM cowlings with a substitute application of a medium blue paint. This particular procedure was quickly abandoned when it was determined that there was insufficient contract between either finish to be functional as a group marker.

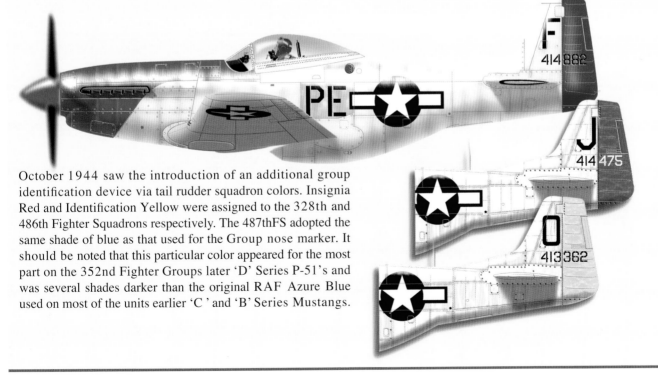

As was the case with many other units within the 8th Air Force, the 352ndFG adopted the use of a bar-code system as a means of identifying duplicate assigned aircraft. This particular devise was positioned below the call letter in all Group applications regardless of the location of the call-letter.

In May of 1944 the 352ndFG selected an RAF Azure Blue shade of paint to replace the original medium blue Group color. To enhance the visibility factor of this new color a sweep back pattern as depicted above was introduced as the official 352nd Fighter Group nose marker. With the introduction of D-Day Invasion Stripes later that month, the 328th and 487th Fighter Squadrons relocated their aircrafts call letters to the tail fin while at the same time the 486th elected to reposition this same symbol just above the wing root and slightly back from the exhaust cutout. This application was short-lived however and by late June the 486th FS had conformed to its sister squadrons and relegated their wayward call-letter on the tail fin as well.

October 1944 saw the introduction of an additional group identification device via tail rudder squadron colors. Insignia Red and Identification Yellow were assigned to the 328th and 486th Fighter Squadrons respectively. The 487thFS adopted the same shade of blue as that used for the Group nose marker. It should be noted that this particular color appeared for the most part on the 352nd Fighter Groups later 'D' Series P-51's and was several shades darker than the original RAF Azure Blue used on most of the units earlier 'C' and 'B' Series Mustangs.

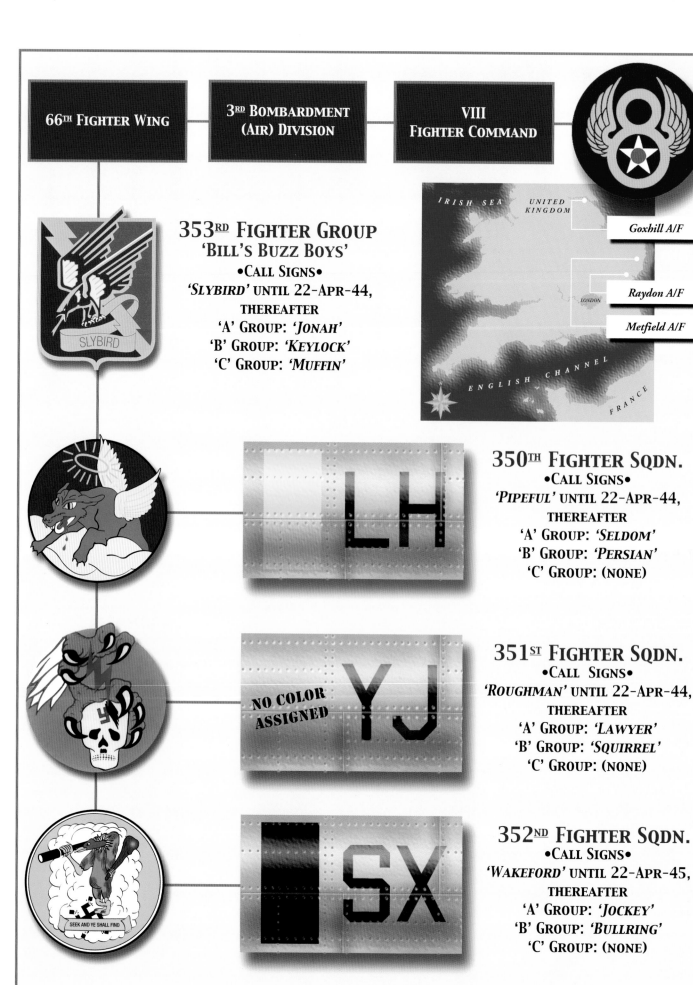

66TH FIGHTER WING

3RD BOMBARDMENT (AIR) DIVISION

VIII FIGHTER COMMAND

IRISH SEA
UNITED KINGDOM

Goxhill A/F

Raydon A/F

Metfield A/F

LONDON

ENGLISH CHANNEL

FRANCE

N

353RD FIGHTER GROUP
'BILL'S BUZZ BOYS'
•CALL SIGNS•
'SLYBIRD' UNTIL 22-APR-44,
THEREAFTER
'A' GROUP: 'JONAH'
'B' GROUP: 'KEYLOCK'
'C' GROUP: 'MUFFIN'

SLYBIRD

350TH FIGHTER SQDN.
•CALL SIGNS•
'PIPEFUL' UNTIL 22-APR-44,
THEREAFTER
'A' GROUP: 'SELDOM'
'B' GROUP: 'PERSIAN'
'C' GROUP: (NONE)

LH

351ST FIGHTER SQDN.
•CALL SIGNS•
'ROUGHMAN' UNTIL 22-APR-44,
THEREAFTER
'A' GROUP: 'LAWYER'
'B' GROUP: 'SQUIRREL'
'C' GROUP: (NONE)

NO COLOR ASSIGNED

YJ

352ND FIGHTER SQDN.
•CALL SIGNS•
'WAKEFORD' UNTIL 22-APR-45,
THEREAFTER
'A' GROUP: 'JOCKEY'
'B' GROUP: 'BULLRING'
'C' GROUP: (NONE)

SEEK AND YE SHALL FIND

SX

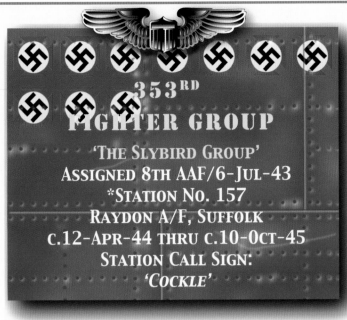

353RD FIGHTER GROUP

'THE SLYBIRD GROUP'
ASSIGNED 8TH AAF/6-JUL-43
*STATION NO. 157
RAYDON A/F, SUFFOLK
C.12-APR-44 THRU C.10-0CT-45
STATION CALL SIGN:
'COCKLE'

What at first glance might appear to be another photograph of a 350thFS P-47 turns out to be a quite interesting image insofar as unit markings are concerned. The diamond pattern is easily discernible on this ships cowling, what is not as noticeable are the additional diamond applications painted on this aircrafts trim tabs. There is an additional diamond motif affixed to the rudder hinge, small and hard to see but there nevertheless. Just how wide spread this type of application was, if at all, is currently unknown. The same applies for the exact significance of these markings although it is *surmised,* based upon the history of this particular aircraft, that these markings may have had a connection with the flight leader status of the pilot.

CAMPAIGNS

• AIR OFFENSIVE-EUROPE • NORMANDY •
• NORTHERN FRANCE • RHINELAND •
• ARDENNES-ALSACE • CENTRAL EUROPE •

* Prior to Raydon the 353rdFG was stationed at the former home of the RAF Group Bomber Command, Goxhill A/F (Station No.345) 7Jun43 thru 3Aug44. Goxhill or 'Goat Hill' as it was nicknamed by AAF personal, was the first airfield to be converted for USAAF use. The 353rdFG was next assigned to Metfield A/F (Station No.366, call sign 'Boyhood'), which would be the Groups home from 3Aug43 until 12Apr44.

None of the combat insignia adopted by the three squadrons comprising the 353rd Fighter Group were officially approved by the AAF. These 'in-house' designs were by no means unique among American fighter units but it is somewhat unusual in this case given the 353rdFGs early deployment to England. As a rule, insignia remained unofficial with units arriving late to the ETO simply due to the fact that the war ended, and this before the normally slow approval process caught up to the preponderance of submission requests. Continuity of image was one of the major drawbacks to these unapproved squadron and group designs as evidenced by the composite image to the right. This image contains three similar yet very different visuals the same squadron insignia, that of the 350th. How does one then select a specific image that best represents a given unit? It is not always easy but the selection was simplified in this case by the fact that we have an excellent photo's of the man responsible for the design of his squadron's insignia wearing a patch of same on his A2 flight jacket. In spite of the fact that the photo of the 350thFS Op's Room clearly shows the insignia to the immediate right, the pilot, then Lt.Dwight Blickenstaff who did in fact design the 350thFS insignia, has clearly affixed to his jacket the insignia overlapping his photograph.

REPUBLIC P-47 'THUNDERBOLT'
c. JUL'43-NOV'44

All of the 353rd Fighter Groups original allocation of P-47s were delivered with the standard two-color factory applied paint scheme. As such the squadron codes and individual aircraft call letters were affixed with white paint in compliance with the VIII Fighter Command directive of 15Jun43. SD110 Squadron codes were assigned to the Group shortly after that units arrival in Great Britain. White QIMs were also present on all of the 353rd Fighter Groups original combat aircraft.

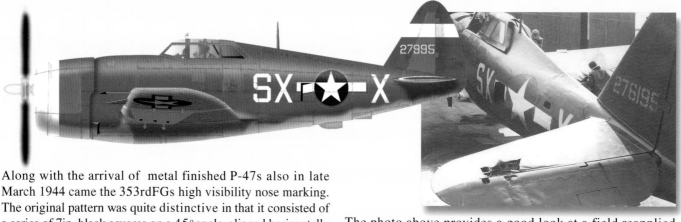

Along with the arrival of metal finished P-47s also in late March 1944 came the 353rdFGs high visibility nose marking. The original pattern was quite distinctive in that it consisted of a series of 7in. black squares on a 45° angle, aligned horizontally over an Identification Yellow background. The visual impact of this configuration was impressive and it is unknown exactly why this was later modified to a 90° square rectangular pattern.

The photo above provides a good look at a field reapplied tail number resplendent with unfilled stencil lines. This was often the case when the original factory applied numbers were replaced under combat conditions.

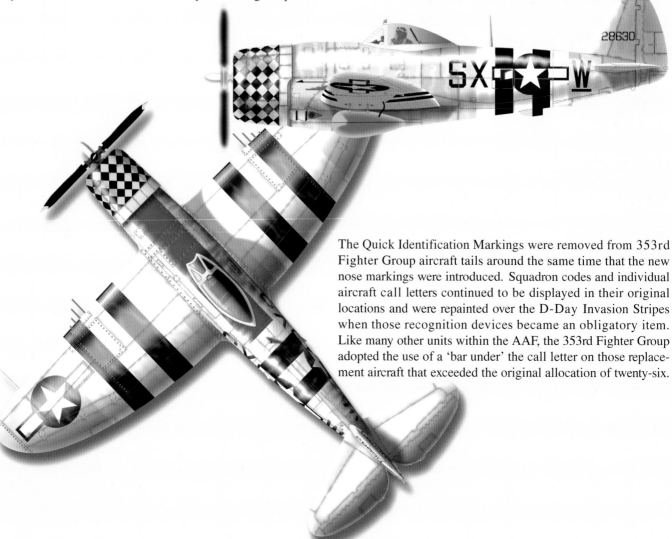

The Quick Identification Markings were removed from 353rd Fighter Group aircraft tails around the same time that the new nose markings were introduced. Squadron codes and individual aircraft call letters continued to be displayed in their original locations and were repainted over the D-Day Invasion Stripes when those recognition devices became an obligatory item. Like many other units within the AAF, the 353rd Fighter Group adopted the use of a 'bar under' the call letter on those replacement aircraft that exceeded the original allocation of twenty-six.

NORTH AMERICAN P-51 'MUSTANG'
c. Oct'44 / VE-Day

The 353rdFG entered combat with their replacement P-51s in late 1944. With the new aircraft came a modified nose pattern, the diamond being replaced with a less striking rectangular motif. Unlike the original P-47 'diamond' pattern, only three rows of a new 6in. yellow & black 'checkerboard' were used to adorn the 353rd's new Mustang cowlings. The spinners were additionally decorated with alternating, and equal rows, of yellow and black and this would remain a constant for the duration of the war. However, the cowling marker would undergo one final modification before VE-Day.

Due to a purported confusion between the nose markings of the 55th Fighter Group, the cowling pattern of the 353rdFG was increased by an additional five rows of 'checks', thus extending the marker back to a point near the end of the exhaust cutout. This final cowling pattern modification was effected in Dec'44.

Shortly after their delivery a number of the Groups Mustangs received a disruptive camouflage pattern of dark green paint, possibly in anticipation of redeployment or partial deployment to forward Allied air bases located on the European Continent.

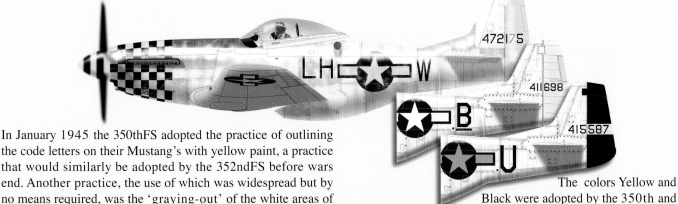

In January 1945 the 350thFS adopted the practice of outlining the code letters on their Mustang's with yellow paint, a practice that would similarly be adopted by the 352ndFS before wars end. Another practice, the use of which was widespread but by no means required, was the 'graying-out' of the white areas of the US National Insignia. This blue & white configuration was believed by many pilots to be a convenient aiming point for enemy gun crews. AAF fighter losses to antiaircraft fire were many times higher than those ships lost in aerial combat.

The colors Yellow and Black were adopted by the 350th and 352nd Fighter Squadrons respectively in November 1944. At this same time the black QIMs were removed from the tail sections. The 351stFS did not utilize an indentifying color. When applying paint to the aircrafts rudders the 352ndFS ground crews simply 'block-masked' out the tail number. 350thFS personnel sometimes elected to use the same masking technique, however, as often as not they would first paint the entire rudder, than reapply the last three numerals of the serial number over the solid Identification Yellow background.

65TH FIGHTER WING	**2ND BOMBARDMENT (AIR) DIVISION**	**VIII FIGHTER COMMAND**	

OUR MIGHT ALWAYS

355TH FIGHTER GROUP
'THE STEEPLE MORDEN STRAFERS'
•CALL SIGNS•
'SUNSHADE' UNTIL 22-APR-44,
THEREAFTER
'A' GROUP: 'UNCLE'
'B' GROUP: 'HORNPIPE'
'C' GROUP: 'BORAX'

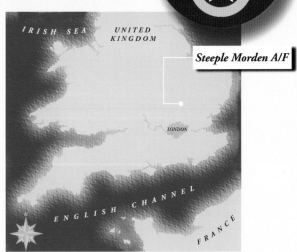

Steeple Morden A/F

354TH FIGHTER SQDN.
•CALL SIGNS•
'HAYWOOD' UNTIL 22-APR-44,
THEREAFTER
'A' GROUP: 'FALCON'
'B' GROUP: 'CHIEFTEN'
'C' GROUP: (NONE)

357TH FIGHTER SQDN.
•CALL SIGNS•
'BLOWBALL' UNTIL 22-APR-44,
THEREAFTER
'A' GROUP: 'CUSTARD'
'B' GROUP: 'MOSES'
'C' GROUP: (NONE)

358TH FIGHTER SQDN.
•CALL SIGNS•
'TROOPTRAIN' UNTIL 22-APR-45,
THEREAFTER
'A' GROUP: 'BENTLEY'
'B' GROUP: 'BEEHIVE'
'C' GROUP: (NONE)

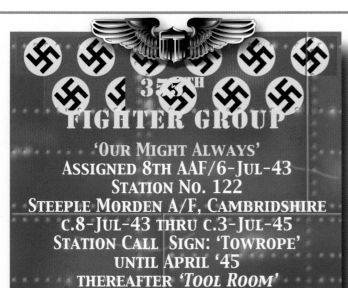

355TH FIGHTER GROUP

'OUR MIGHT ALWAYS'
ASSIGNED 8TH AAF/6-JUL-43
STATION NO. 122
STEEPLE MORDEN A/F, CAMBRIDSHIRE
c.8-JUL-43 THRU c.3-JUL-45
STATION CALL SIGN: 'TOWROPE'
UNTIL APRIL '45
THEREAFTER 'TOOL ROOM'

CAMPAIGNS
• AIR OFFENSIVE-EUROPE • NORMANDY •
• NORTHERN FRANCE • RHINELAND •
• ARDENNES-ALSACE • CENTRAL EUROPE •

Like most AAF pilots of the era, 355th Fighter Group pilots utilized a wide assortment of images when it came to applying victory symbols to their aircraft as this group of photos clearly illustrates.

These two photos illustrate most prevalent method of recording mission tallies on individual aircraft within the 479th Fighter Group. A horizontal configuration of bomb and broom symbols were applied with yellow or white paint on camouflaged aircraft, while black or red was used on the metal finished ships. As of this writing, no photographic evidence has been found to confirm the use of additional mission symbols (i.e., locomotives, top hats, etc.) by the 355th Fighter Group squadrons.

REPUBLIC P-47 'THUNDERBOLT'
C. JUL'43-NOV'44

The majority of combat P-47s flown by the 353rdFG consisted of the standard two-color camouflaged variety. The UK/QIMs were applied to these aircraft shortly after their arrival within the Group, followed shortly thereafter by the squadron fuselage codes which were assigned in August of 1943. In addition to the fuselage call letter, many of the Groups aircraft displayed a duplicate call-letter in black paint on the lower engine cowling, as seen in the wartime photograph to the immediate right.

When replacement aircraft began to exceed the 355th's original allotment of twenty-six per squadron, the Group adopted the policy of applying a horizontal bar directly beneath the call letter as a means of identifying duplicates. This policy would carry over when the 355th ultimately converted to the Mustang.

As was typical with many USAAF during this early period, there was little to distinguish 355th Fighter Group aircraft from similarly equipped US units. Like many other Thunderbolt groups, an oversized national emblem (60in. diameter vs. a standard 40in.) was often applied to the wing surfaces, especially the undersides, in the hope that this would minimize the risk of their P-47s being erroneously identified by allied aircraft spotters and often nervous gun crews as a German Focke-Wulf /Fw 190 fighter.

356TH FIGHTER GROUP

ASSIGNED 8TH AAF/25-AUG-43
1.) STATION No. 345
GOXHILL A/F, LINCOLNSHIRE
c.27-AUG-43 THRU c.5-OCT-43
STATION CALL SIGN: (UNKNOWN)
2.) STATION No. 369
MARTLESHAM HEATH A/F, SUFFOLK
c.5-OCT-43 THRU c.2-NOV-45
STATION CALL SIGN: *'RECOUNT'*

CAMPAIGNS
- AIR OFFENSIVE-EUROPE • NORMANDY •
- NORTHERN FRANCE • RHINELAND •
- ARDENNES-ALSACE • CENTRAL EUROPE •

359TH
FIGHTER SQUADRON

Of the original three combat insignia adopted by the squadrons comprising the 356th Fighter Group, the sole image to remain unchanged throughout the war was that of the 360th Fighter Squadron. The image above belonged to the 359th Fighter Squadron until late 1944, and could have been easily modified to reflect the Groups recent transition from the P-47 Thunderbolt to the P-51 Mustang, but this course of action was not followed. The history of the two images representing the 361st Fighter Squadron is somewhat cloudy at the time of this writing. The design at left was displayed by that unit at one time and is in fact sometimes used today in representing this squadron. The design depicted on the facing page however was submitted to the Army for approval in early 1945 and the original art work remains on file in offical USAAF archives.

361ST
FIGHTER SQUADRON

A close examination of the photograph at lower right (once the bar area of the 359th Fighter Squadron) reveals that it was probably taken sometime after the 359thFG had converted to the P-51 Mustang. As noted in the accompanying text above, the 359thFS was more or less obliged to recreate or at least modify their original insignia due to the Thunderbolt image incorporated within that design. For whatever reasons, the former course of action was selected and the replacement was the slingshot wielding chickenhawk depicted on the facing page. The new 359thFS image as well as the replacement 361st Fighter Squadron insignia were both submitted for approval at about the same time, in early 1945, thus narrowing down this photos time frame.

Although the enlarged inset has nothing to do with insignia or markings, the creative use of 'available materials' warranted a special notice. This puts an entirely new twist on the familiar biblical '*swords into plow shares*' proverb.

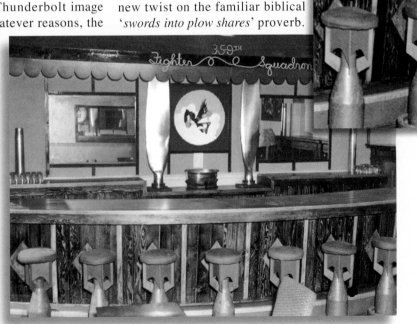

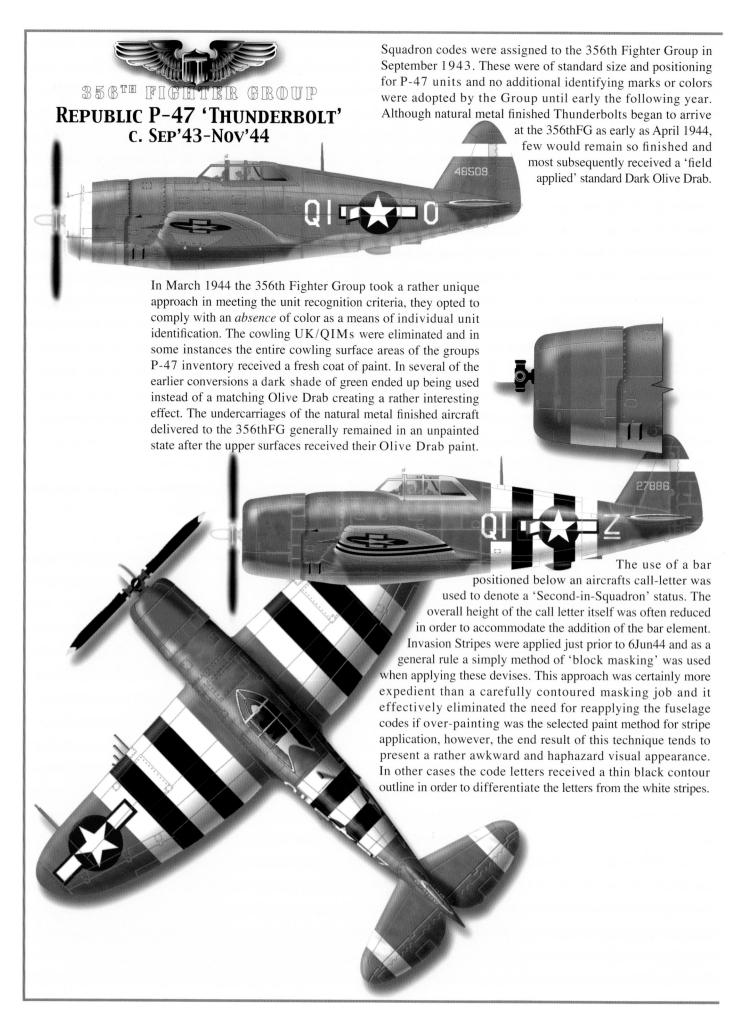

356TH FIGHTER GROUP
REPUBLIC P-47 'THUNDERBOLT'
c. SEP'43-NOV'44

Squadron codes were assigned to the 356th Fighter Group in September 1943. These were of standard size and positioning for P-47 units and no additional identifying marks or colors were adopted by the Group until early the following year. Although natural metal finished Thunderbolts began to arrive at the 356thFG as early as April 1944, few would remain so finished and most subsequently received a 'field applied' standard Dark Olive Drab.

In March 1944 the 356th Fighter Group took a rather unique approach in meeting the unit recognition criteria, they opted to comply with an *absence* of color as a means of individual unit identification. The cowling UK/QIMs were eliminated and in some instances the entire cowling surface areas of the groups P-47 inventory received a fresh coat of paint. In several of the earlier conversions a dark shade of green ended up being used instead of a matching Olive Drab creating a rather interesting effect. The undercarriages of the natural metal finished aircraft delivered to the 356thFG generally remained in an unpainted state after the upper surfaces received their Olive Drab paint.

The use of a bar positioned below an aircrafts call-letter was used to denote a 'Second-in-Squadron' status. The overall height of the call letter itself was often reduced in order to accommodate the addition of the bar element. Invasion Stripes were applied just prior to 6Jun44 and as a general rule a simply method of 'block masking' was used when applying these devises. This approach was certainly more expedient than a carefully contoured masking job and it effectively eliminated the need for reapplying the fuselage codes if over-painting was the selected paint method for stripe application, however, the end result of this technique tends to present a rather awkward and haphazard visual appearance. In other cases the code letters received a thin black contour outline in order to differentiate the letters from the white stripes.

NORTH AMERICAN P-51 'MUSTANG'
c. NOV'44 / VE-DAY

The 356th Fighter Group received their first 'D' Series P-51 in October of 1944 and entered combat with these the following month. Initially these aircraft bore no distinguishing marks save the original squadron codes handed down from the P-47's. Unlike its predecessors, none of the 356thFG Mustangs would receive the familiar two-color camouflage paint configuration.

By the end of November, early December of 1944, the 356thFG adopted high profile color markings with a vengeance. All P-51 Mustang spinners received an overall coat of medium blue paint. The area just forward the prop cutouts was equally divided into 2in. segments of alternating red and blue horizontal color bands. The forward fuselage received an overall coat of red paint in the configuration shown above. This was accented with a series of elongated triangles, approximately 4in.x 8in. of the same blue shade as that used on the spinners. The exact application of this diamond pattern varied somewhat from one aircraft to another, but the overall effect created a very dynamic unit recognition pattern which was a far cry from the Groups initial lackluster days with the P-47 Thunderbolt.

In January 1945 all 356th Fighter Group Mustangs main canopy frames began to be adorned in squadron colors. These areas also came to be the location of choice of many of the Group's pilots for displaying individual victory or 'Kill Marks'.

The 356th Fighter Groups squadrons began painting the aircraft's rudders in their respective colors, January 1945. At first the black QIM tail stripe was not over-painted but masked out prior to this addition, however this practice was short-lived and the QIM's were than simply over-painted. Eventually this issue was solved when the use of QIM's were unilaterally discontinued altogether. Replacement aircraft lacked these markings and were eventually removed from the Groups older inventory. The 359th and 361st Fighter Squadrons repainted the rudder digits in black, while the 360thFS initially 'block-masked' these same numerals prior to painting the rudders. This practice too was short-lived and the 360thFS soon adopted its sister squadrons procedure of reinstating these rudder numbers in black after the squadron paint application.

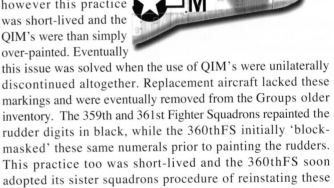

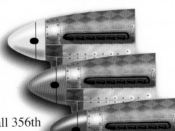

Beginning in February 1945 all 356th FG Mustang spinners were repainted in proper squadron colors. The overriding factor behind this change was the additional time required to apply the original Group striped pattern. This modification was undoubtedly welcomed by the Groups already heavily burdened ground maintenance crews, not to mention that squadron recognition became further enhanced.

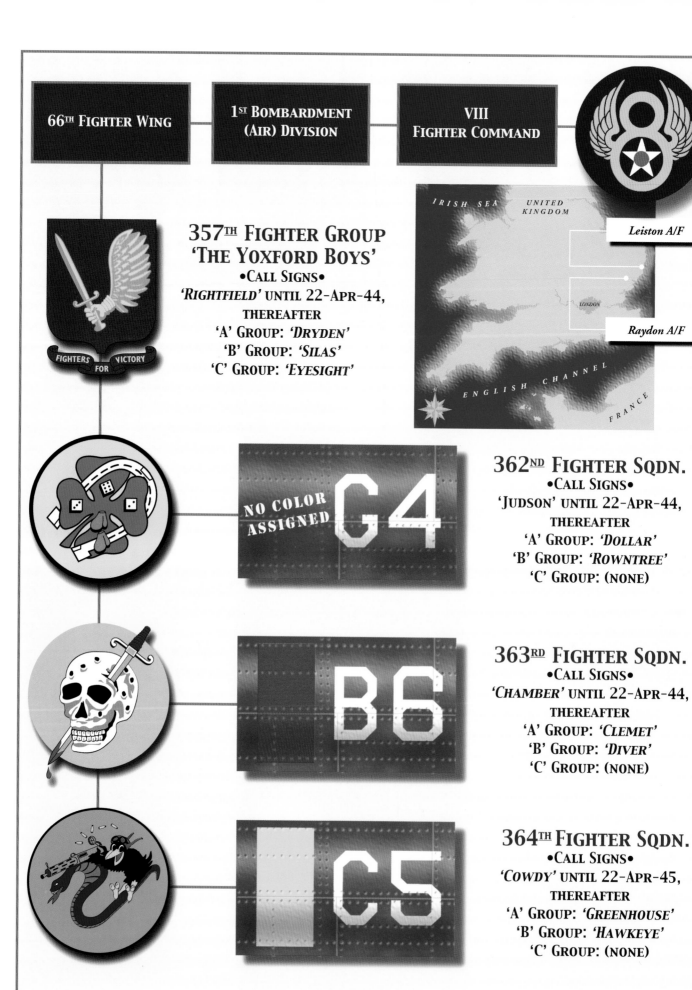

66TH FIGHTER WING — **1ST BOMBARDMENT (AIR) DIVISION** — **VIII FIGHTER COMMAND**

357TH FIGHTER GROUP 'THE YOXFORD BOYS'
•CALL SIGNS•
'RIGHTFIELD' UNTIL 22-APR-44,
THEREAFTER
'A' GROUP: *'DRYDEN'*
'B' GROUP: *'SILAS'*
'C' GROUP: *'EYESIGHT'*

IRISH SEA UNITED KINGDOM

Leiston A/F

LONDON

Raydon A/F

ENGLISH CHANNEL

FRANCE

FIGHTERS FOR VICTORY

NO COLOR ASSIGNED **G4**

362ND FIGHTER SQDN.
•CALL SIGNS•
'JUDSON' UNTIL 22-APR-44,
THEREAFTER
'A' GROUP: *'DOLLAR'*
'B' GROUP: *'ROWNTREE'*
'C' GROUP: (NONE)

B6

363RD FIGHTER SQDN.
•CALL SIGNS•
'CHAMBER' UNTIL 22-APR-44,
THEREAFTER
'A' GROUP: *'CLEMET'*
'B' GROUP: *'DIVER'*
'C' GROUP: (NONE)

C5

364TH FIGHTER SQDN.
•CALL SIGNS•
'COWDY' UNTIL 22-APR-45,
THEREAFTER
'A' GROUP: *'GREENHOUSE'*
'B' GROUP: *'HAWKEYE'*
'C' GROUP: (NONE)

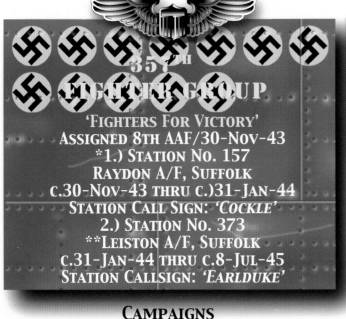

357TH FIGHTER GROUP

'FIGHTERS FOR VICTORY'
ASSIGNED 8TH AAF/30-NOV-43
*1.) STATION NO. 157
RAYDON A/F, SUFFOLK
C.30-NOV-43 THRU C.)31-JAN-44
STATION CALL SIGN: 'COCKLE'
2.) STATION NO. 373
**LEISTON A/F, SUFFOLK
C.31-JAN-44 THRU C.8-JUL-45
STATION CALLSIGN: 'EARLDUKE'

CAMPAIGNS

• AIR OFFENSIVE-EUROPE • NORMANDY •
• NORTHERN FRANCE • RHINELAND •
• ARDENNES-ALSACE • CENTRAL EUROPE •

*While the 357thFG was stationed at Raydon A/F, the Group had been issued its squadron codes, and at the time was serving with the 9thAAF. This was one of the first units within the 8thAAF to adopt SD110 squadron codes which departed from the previously standard 'double letter' system of identification.

** Leiston was also known as Theberton/Saxmundham A/F.

The 362ndFS appears to have made good use of their combat insignia as evidenced by the images directly above. Research also turned up similar photographic records depicting the use of the 363rdFS insignia. All photos were taken at Leiston A/F.

Although the main canopy frame was the preferred location with many AAF pilots of the P-51 when it came to applying their individual 'kill marks', the men of the 357thFG tended to carry on with their custom of displaying these images on the mid-fuselage area of their Mustangs. The Group had begun combat operations with the 'B' and 'C' series P-51s which did not offer a large main canopy frame as an option, thus all victory marks were applied to the fuselage by necessity. This procedure seems to have become somewhat of a 357thFG tradition, which would be carried over to the later model 'bubble top' replacement Mustangs.

Victory or 'kill' marks within the 8thAAF ran the gambit from a simple outline of the German Balkenkreuz to very elaborate imagery such as that depicted on the 362nd FS Mustang in the photo to the immediate left which is a stylized Luftwaffe insignia.

NORTH AMERICAN P-51 'MUSTANG'
c. NOV'43 - DEC'44

The original consignment of 'B' / 'C' series P-51's allocated to the 357thFG bore a factory applied two-color paint scheme of Olive Drab over Neutral Grey. When the 357th began receiving replacement Mustangs that lacked this camouflage (April '44) the Group adopted a policy of painting all natural metal finished combat aircraft with their own two-color camouflage paint scheme. The colors used by the 357th varied considerably due to a wide assortment of supply sources. The upper colors ranged from O.D. to a dark green. The under surfaces ran the gambit from a standard U.S. Neutral Grey to a light grey. In June of the same year, a few of the Groups Mustangs received a partial green paint treatment to the upper wing and top fuselage/tail plane surfaces. This often included the full rudder surface area. Another handful simply had the antiglare panel extended to the rear of the canopy and ultimately intersected the base of the vertical stabilizer.

With the introduction of Invasion Stripes in early June 1944 the squadron codes were either masked-out prior to the application of the D-Day Stripes or removed entirely and later reinstated further forward on the fuselage using the original white paint. The photo below shows a combination 'contour / block masking' of the codes while the adjacent illustration depicts a typical repositioning application. A third, less used option, was 'image masking' the codes when applying the Invasion Stripes and than adding a contrasting black or white contour outline to these codes once the stripes had been applied and masking removed.

The original 357th Mustangs displayed the standard white QIM markings until the group adopted its dual color high visibility nose markings in March of '44. When Invasion Stripes were ordered immediately prior to the D-Day Landings, the 357th complied with the directive with one quite notable exception; the upper wing surfaces of all the Groups aircraft continued to carry the original white UK/QIM stripes instead of the normal two-color Invasion Stripes. Just how this came to pass is uncertain today but it is highly unlikely that such a course of action was an arbitrary decision at Group level. For whatever reason it would appear that the 357thFG received an exemption insofar as the top wing surface D-Day Invasion Stripes were concerned.

Very early on the 357thFG adopted the use of a horizontal bar in conjunction with individual aircraft call letters to designate the 'Second-in-Squadron' status of any replacement ship exceeding the Groups original allocation of twenty-six P-51's. Although there were a few early examples of this devise being placed *below* the call letter, by far the majority of these bars were located *above* this letter. It is interesting to note that within the 357th Fighter Group, The 362ndFS left a good portion of the fuselage code stencil lines unfilled and a majority of the 363rdFS were likewise left unpainted. The 364thFS on the other hand rarely left any of these stencil lines unfilled when applying the fuselage codes to their aircraft.

NORTH AMERICAN P-51 'MUSTANG'
C.JAN'44–V/E DAY

By the beginning of April 1944 the 357thFG was well on its way to completing the application of the Groups recently assigned high visibility nose markings to all squadron aircraft. As illustrated below, this marking consisted of a two-color spinner divided into three equal parts, which proceeded two rows of alternating 6in. (approx.) red and yellow rectangles that entirely encircled the forward fuselage engine cowling.

The application of two-color camouflaged paint schemes to 357thFG Mustangs (as depicted below) had ceased by early October 1944. By January 1945 all such paint had been in fact removed and the 357th displayed metal finishes until wars end.

The wartime photo immediately above is yet another example of the variation in marking applications that occurred within the 8thAAF under combat conditions. Note the uneven division of this aircraft's spinner, and this in spite of a clear directive calling for this very devise to be divided into three *equal* parts.

In October 1944 the 363rd and 364th Fighter Squadrons adopted colors to be applied to their aircraft's rudders to assist in unit recognition. These were Insignia Red for the 363rd and Identification Yellow was assigned to the 364th. The rudder digits on 364thFS aircraft were repainted utilizing the original black color while these same numbers were reinstated in both black *and* yellow on 363rdFS applications. The 362nd Fighter Squadron did not adopt an identifying color and their P-51's rudders remained in either Olive Drab, or later, natural metal finishes until the end of hostilities in the European Theater.

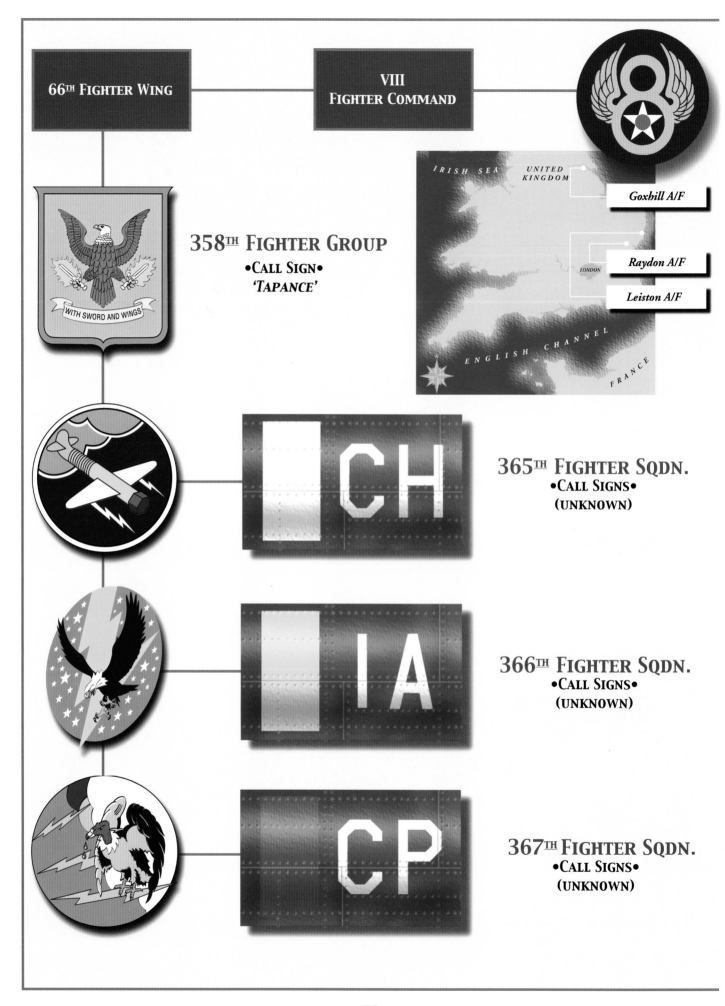

66th Fighter Wing

VIII Fighter Command

Goxhill A/F

Raydon A/F

Leiston A/F

358th Fighter Group
•Call Sign•
'Tapance'

WITH SWORD AND WINGS

365th Fighter Sqdn.
•Call Signs•
(unknown)

366th Fighter Sqdn.
•Call Signs•
(unknown)

367th Fighter Sqdn.
•Call Signs•
(unknown)

358TH FIGHTER GROUP
'WITH SWORD AND WINGS'
ASSIGNED 8TH AAF/20-OCT-43
1.) STATION No. 345
GOXHILL A/F, LINCOLNSHIRE
c.20-OCT-43 THRU c.28-NOV-43
STATION CALL SIGN: (UNKNOWN)
2.) STATION No. 373
LEISTON A/F, SUFFOLK
c.29-NOV-43 THRU c.28-JAN-44
STATION CALLSIGN: 'EARLDUKE'
*3.) STATION No. 157
RAYDON A/F, SUFFOLK
c.31-JAN-44 THRU c.12-APR-44
STATION CALL SIGN: 'COCKLE'

CAMPAIGNS
• AMERICAN THEATER • AIR OFFENSIVE-EUROPE •
• NORMANDY • NORTHERN FRANCE • RHINELAND •
• ARDENNES-ALSACE • CENTRAL EUROPE •

It has been noted earlier that the 357th Fighter Group was somewhat unique among 8thAAF Fighter units in that its squadrons displayed the *letter-number* combination squadron code designations that had been assigned prior to the 357th's transfer from the 9thAAF. Conversely, even after transferring to the 9thAAF, the 358thFG squadrons continued to carry the *double-letter* codes that had been assigned to them while with the Eighth AF. These codes would remain unchanged throughout the remainder of the war.

The squadron colors depicted on the facing page would eventually be used on each of the respective squadrons tail rudders and engine cowlings as tactical unit markings. It should be noted however that unlike the squadron codes, these colors were not displayed by the 358th FG squadrons until after that units transfer to the Ninth Air Force. In regards to the individual combat insignia displayed by each unit, the following information is available; neither the 358th Fighter Group nor the 365th Fighter Squadron insignia were ever officially approved for use. The 366th and 367th Fighter Squadron insignia on the other hand were both approved by the Army's Board of Heraldry on 6Sep43 and 1Mar44 respectively. While these dates confirm that the latter two insignia were in use, to date no written or photographic evidence has been located that would verify whether or not the first two *unofficial* designs were in use during the brief time that the 358th Fighter Group was assigned to the 8thAAF at either Leiston or Goxhill.

The 358th Fighter Groups tenure with the Eighth Air Force was brief by any standards, less than three full months. Shortly after completing their UK training, the 358thFG was 'swapped' to the Ninth Air Force in exchange for the 357th Fighter Group. This was a mutually advantageous arrangement due to the specific needs of each air force. The 8thAAF was in constant need of additional fighter escort for its ever- increasing strategic bombing campaign against the Third Reich while the 9thAAF was busy stepping up its tactical assaults over Continental Europe in preparation for the pending D-Day landings. The 357th Fighter Group was equipped with P-51 Mustangs, the consummate high altitude US escort fighter, while the 358th Fighter Group flew the rugged P-47 which was ideally suited to the low level ground attack campaign than being conducted by the Ninth.

*A final change of UK postings occurred on 13Apr44 when the 358thFG was transferred to Station No.411 / High Halden A/F, in Kent. After a brief stay at High Halden, the 358th was moved to the Continent where it would remain until wars end.

66TH FIGHTER WING AND 67TH FIGHTER WING — **2ND BOMBARDMENT (AIR) DIVISION** — **VIII FIGHTER COMMAND**

359TH FIGHTER GROUP
'THE UNICORNS'
•CALL SIGNS•
'WALLPAINT' UNTIL 22-APR-44,
THEREAFTER
'A' GROUP: 'CHAIRMAN'
'B' GROUP: 'CAVETOP'
'C' GROUP: 'RAGTIME'

East Wretham A/F

368TH FIGHTER SQDN.
•CALL SIGNS•
'BEESNEST' UNTIL 2-JAN-44,
'JACKSON' UNTIL 22-APR-44
THEREAFTER
'A' GROUP: 'JIGGER'
'B' GROUP: 'HANDY'
'C' GROUP: (NONE)

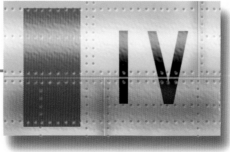

369TH FIGHTER SQDN.
•CALL SIGNS•
'TIRETREAD' UNTIL 22-APR-44,
THEREAFTER
'A' GROUP: 'TINPLATE'
'B' GROUP: 'EARNEST'
'C' GROUP: (NONE)

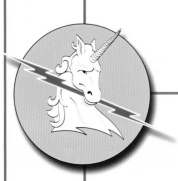

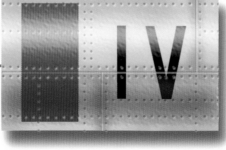

370TH FIGHTER SQDN.
•CALL SIGNS•
'WHEELER' UNTIL 22-APR-44,
THEREAFTER
'A' GROUP: 'REDCROSS'
'B' GROUP: 'ROLLO'
'C' GROUP: (NONE)

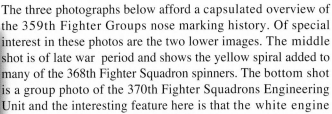

359TH FIGHTER GROUP

'CUM LEONE'
ASSIGNED 8TH AAF/19-OCT-43
STATION NO. 133
EAST WRENTHAM A/F, NORFOLK
C.19-OCT-43 THRU C.2-NOV-45
STATION CALL SIGN:
'WOODBROOK'

CAMPAIGNS
• AIR OFFENSIVE-EUROPE • NORMANDY •
• NORTHERN FRANCE • RHINELAND •
• ARDENNES-ALSACE • CENTRAL EUROPE •

The three photographs below afford a capsulated overview of the 359th Fighter Groups nose marking history. Of special interest in these photos are the two lower images. The middle shot is of late war period and shows the yellow spiral added to many of the 368th Fighter Squadron spinners. The bottom shot is a group photo of the 370th Fighter Squadrons Engineering Unit and the interesting feature here is that the white engine cowling should have been repainted Light Green by the time the 359th Fighter Group had received its first P-51s.

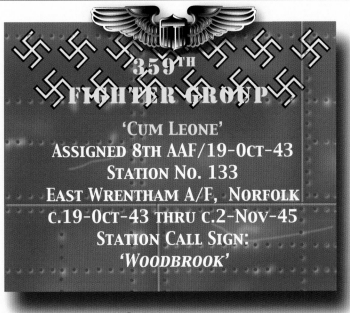

Other than the change in squadron codes when the 4th Fighter Group made the transition from British Spitfires to Thunderbolts, this is the only other known modification to a squadron code within the Eighth Air Force during World War II. The exact reason for this change is uncertain today but what is certain is that the other two squadron codes remained intact as first issued, the 370th being the only effected unit within the 359th Fighter Group. Note the red outlined fuselage codes in the lower photo. This practice became quite common, although not standardized, among the 370th Fighter Squadron.

Flight Leader Rene Burtner (left) and two fellow pilots posed in front of Butners P-51D, ' Hubert' / IV-D / a/c number 472366. Note the Command Stripes on the dorsal fin fillet used to designate Burtner as 'D' Flight Leader of the 369th FtrSqdn / 359thFtrGrp.

REPUBLIC P-47 'THUNDERBOLT'
C. OCT'43-MAY'44

Although the 359thFG did not become officially operational until mid-December of 1943, many of its pilots had flown combat sorties with another 8thAAF fighter group beginning shortly after the air eschelons arrival in England earlier in October of the same year. Individual squadron codes had been assigned to the 359thFG one month earlier and these were displayed on all Group P-47s in the prescribed manner for all P-47 units within Great Britian.

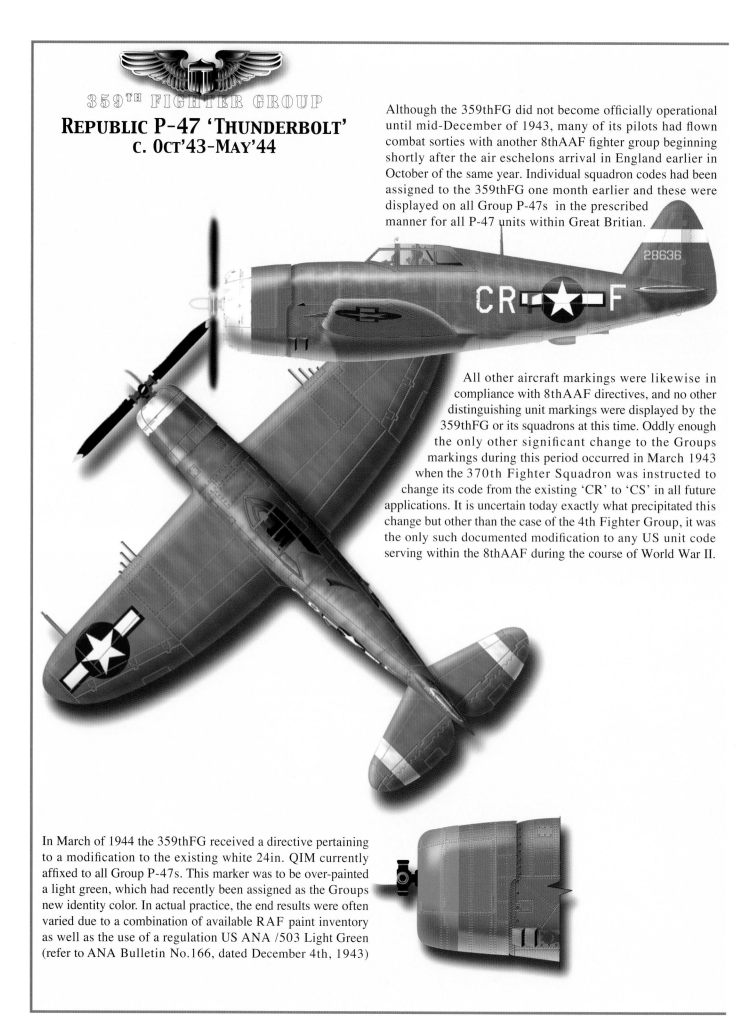

All other aircraft markings were likewise in compliance with 8thAAF directives, and no other distinguishing unit markings were displayed by the 359thFG or its squadrons at this time. Oddly enough the only other significant change to the Groups markings during this period occurred in March 1943 when the 370th Fighter Squadron was instructed to change its code from the existing 'CR' to 'CS' in all future applications. It is uncertain today exactly what precipitated this change but other than the case of the 4th Fighter Group, it was the only such documented modification to any US unit code serving within the 8thAAF during the course of World War II.

In March of 1944 the 359thFG received a directive pertaining to a modification to the existing white 24in. QIM currently affixed to all Group P-47s. This marker was to be over-painted a light green, which had recently been assigned as the Groups new identity color. In actual practice, the end results were often varied due to a combination of available RAF paint inventory as well as the use of a regulation US ANA /503 Light Green (refer to ANA Bulletin No.166, dated December 4th, 1943)

NORTH AMERICAN P-51 'MUSTANG'
c. MAY'44 –VE DAY

After receipt of their replacement P-51s, most of which were delivered with a two-color camouflage paint scheme, the same light green paint shade used on the Groups P-47s was selected to decorate the spinner and initial 24 inches of all 359thFG Mustang engine cowlings. Numerous aircraft carried the wing and tail QIMs for some time after their 23Mar44 removal date.

As natural metal finished P-51s began to arrive, the nose areas originally received the same light green shade as previously applied to the camouflaged aircraft. It was quickly discovered however that this particular shade of paint lacked sufficient contrast against the metal finishes to be effective as a unit marker. As a result, by mid summer 1944, a medium green paint was chosen as the replacement color on all 359thFG aircraft. The nose paint tended to fade rather quickly resulting in a wide assortment of green color shades within the Group.

At about the same time the 368th Fighter Squadron adopted (albeit unofficially) the custom of painting its rudder trim tabs in the same green shade as that used on nose applications. A limited number of natural metal finished Mustangs received a disruptive camouflage application of dark green paint to the upper surface areas of the wings, horizontal stabilizers and emphannage. For whatever reason, many 359thFG aircraft continued to display the black QIMs on the horizontal stabilizers long after these were ordered removed.

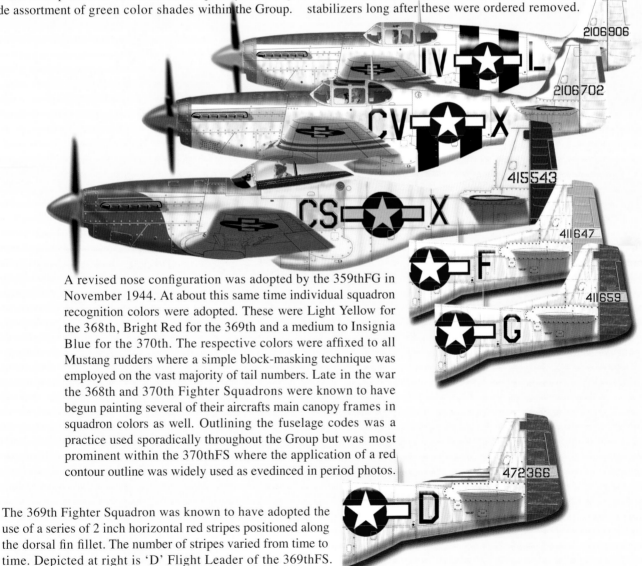

A revised nose configuration was adopted by the 359thFG in November 1944. At about this same time individual squadron recognition colors were adopted. These were Light Yellow for the 368th, Bright Red for the 369th and a medium to Insignia Blue for the 370th. The respective colors were affixed to all Mustang rudders where a simple block-masking technique was employed on the vast majority of tail numbers. Late in the war the 368th and 370th Fighter Squadrons were known to have begun painting several of their aircrafts main canopy frames in squadron colors as well. Outlining the fuselage codes was a practice used sporadically throughout the Group but was most prominent within the 370thFS where the application of a red contour outline was widely used as evedinced in period photos.

The 369th Fighter Squadron was known to have adopted the use of a series of 2 inch horizontal red stripes positioned along the dorsal fin fillet. The number of stripes varied from time to time. Depicted at right is 'D' Flight Leader of the 369thFS.

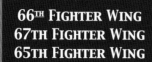

66TH FIGHTER WING
67TH FIGHTER WING
65TH FIGHTER WING

2ND BOMBARDMENT (AIR) DIVISION

VIII FIGHTER COMMAND

361ST FIGHTER GROUP
'THE YELLOW JACKETS'
•CALL SIGNS•
'WILDCAT' UNTIL 22-APR-44,
THEREAFTER
'A' GROUP: 'CHEERFUL'
LATER 'GLOWBRIGHT'
'B' GROUP: 'MARBLE'
LATER 'FILLY'
'C' GROUP: 'MALTESE'
LATER 'MAGPIE'

Bottisham A/F

Little Walden A/F

374TH FIGHTER SQDN.
•CALL SIGNS•
'HUBBARD' UNTIL 22-APR-44
THEREAFTER
'A' GROUP: 'NOGGIN' LATER 'AMBROSE'
'B' GROUP: 'KINGDOM' LATER 'RIPPER'
'C' GROUP: (NONE)

375TH FIGHTER SQDN.
•CALL SIGNS•
'WABASH' UNTIL 22-APR-44
THEREAFTER
'A' GROUP: 'CADET' LATER 'DECOY'
'B' GROUP: 'DAYDREAM' LATER 'DISHCLOTH'
'C' GROUP: (NONE)

376TH FIGHTER SQDN.
•CALL SIGNS•
'GAYLORD' UNTIL 22-APR-44
THEREAFTER
'A' GROUP: 'TITUS' LATER 'YORKSHIRE'
'B' GROUP: 'STYLE' LATER 'SKYBLUE'
'C' GROUP: (NONE)

361ST
FIGHTER GROUP
ASSIGNED 8TH AAF/30-NOV-43
1.) STATION NO. 374
BOTTISHAM A/F, CAMBRIDGESHIRE
C.30-NOV-43 THRU C.26-SEP-44
STATION CALL SIGN: 'LAKEPRESS'
*2.) STATION NO.165
LITTLE WALDEN A/F, ESSEX
C.26-SEP-44 THRU C.3-NOV-45
STATION CALL SIGN: 'DARKFOLD'

CAMPAIGNS
• AIR OFFENSIVE-EUROPE • NORMANDY •
• NORTHERN FRANCE • RHINELAND •
• ARDENNES-ALSACE • CENTRAL EUROPE •

Of the two photos below the first image illustrates the typical upper surface camouflage 'edging' applied to most of the 361st FG Mustangs in mid 1944. Note that the lead aircraft is the only one in this flight displaying a second pattern high visibility paint scheme making it reasonably certain that this image could be dated from somewhere between July and August of 1944. The second photo shows the application of paint to the top edge of the vertical stabilizer as well as the trim tab and wing tips. This was a widely used practice among the squadron's of the 361st until the application of squadron colors to the rudder areas was adopted in latter October '44.

The 361stFG was transferred briefly (c.Feb-Apr'44) to Station No. A-84 located at Chievres, Belgium. A detachment from the 361st had been dispatched earlier to France (c.Dec'44-Jan'45) in support of Allied ground forces during the Battle of the Bulge.

This photograph depicts an interesting use of the 374th Fighter Squadrons combat insignia. Such applications were commonplace at most U.S. Army airfields but unfortunately, not photo documented nearly enough to suit those of us today interested in the study of this subject.

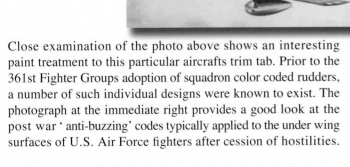

Close examination of the photo above shows an interesting paint treatment to this particular aircrafts trim tab. Prior to the 361st Fighter Groups adoption of squadron color coded rudders, a number of such individual designs were known to exist. The photograph at the immediate right provides a good look at the post war ' anti-buzzing' codes typically applied to the under wing surfaces of U.S. Air Force fighters after cession of hostilities.

361ST FIGHTER GROUP
REPUBLIC P-47 'THUNDERBOLT'
C. DEC'43-MAY'44

A close examination of this photo reveals what appears what could possibly be a camouflage blotching application to the surface area of this 374th Fighter Squadron Thunderbolt. There are however no records located to date that indicate that any of the 361st Fighter Group aircraft received such a camouflage treatment, thus leaving current and future students of this period with yet another unanswered question to explore.

The 361st Fighter Groups original combat inventory had little to distinquish itself from all other Thunderbolt units, except for the individual squadron codes which were issued shortly after the beginning of 1944 and applied in a standard format which conformed to similar units within the Eighth AAF structure.

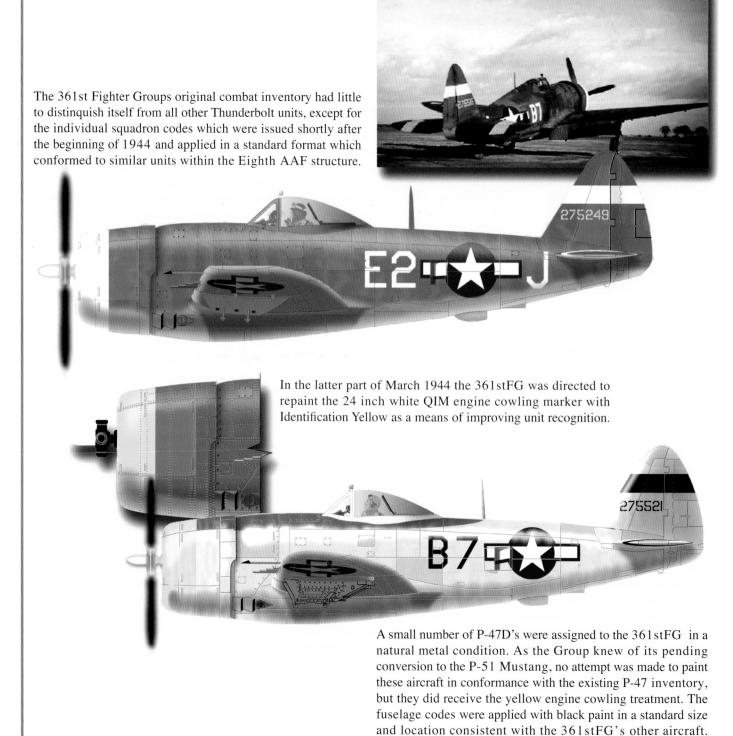

In the latter part of March 1944 the 361stFG was directed to repaint the 24 inch white QIM engine cowling marker with Identification Yellow as a means of improving unit recognition.

A small number of P-47D's were assigned to the 361stFG in a natural metal condition. As the Group knew of its pending conversion to the P-51 Mustang, no attempt was made to paint these aircraft in conformance with the existing P-47 inventory, but they did receive the yellow engine cowling treatment. The fuselage codes were applied with black paint in a standard size and location consistent with the 361stFG's other aircraft.

NORTH AMERICAN P-51 'MUSTANG'
c. MAY'44 / VE-DAY

The original yellow engine cowling pattern was incorporated on the new P-51's and extended forward to include the spinner. Although the vast majority of new P-51 Mustangs delivered to the 361st were of a natural metal finish variety, almost all were to receive an 'edging' application of Dark Green paint to their upper surface areas soon after delivery. The black tail QIM's were removed and the top half of these bands located on the horizontal stabilizers were over-painted and not thereafter reapplied in any form.

The camouflaging treatment included the both upper wing and horizontal stabilizer surface areas. This application of Dark Green was, however often confined to the inner half of the upper wing surface on a good number of these applications. Wing tips as well as trim tabs and the top edges of the tail fin often received a wide assortment of individualized paint applications during the period prior to the assignment of official squadron colors in late October of the same year.

In late July 1944 the original yellow nose pattern was significantly modified to its final configuration. With the adoption of official squadron colors the following October, these colors soon began to appear on wing tips as well as the designated rudder areas. Some canopy frames would also receive a similar paint treatment. Beginning in 1945 it became a standard practice throughout the 361stFG to paint all aircraft wing tips in their respective unit colors:

Insignia Red.................374thFS
Medium Blue...............375thFS
Identification Yellow...376thFS

In most instances the existing aircraft serial number was simply 'block-masked' over prior to the painting of the rudder. In the case of the 376th Fighter Squadron however, there were numerous examples were the rudder digits were over-painted and later reinstated. In these cases the stencil lines might or might not be filled-in after the numerals were re-applied.

All three squadrons within the 361stFG utilized a bar code positioned beneath the individual aircraft call-letter to denote replacements exceeding the original inventory of twenty-six.

| 67ᵀᴴ FIGHTER WING | 1ˢᵀ BOMBARDMENT (AIR) DIVISION | VIII FIGHTER COMMAND |  |

Honington A/F

364ᵀᴴ FIGHTER GROUP
•CALL SIGNS•
'A' GROUP: *'SUNHAT'*
'B' GROUP: *'WEEKDAY'*
'C' GROUP: *'HARLOP'*

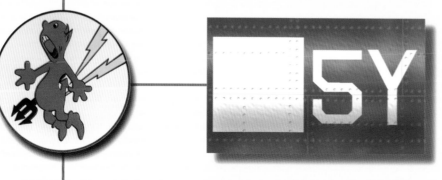

383ᴿᴰ FIGHTER SQDN.
•CALL SIGNS•
'A' GROUP: *'ESCORT'*
'B' GROUP: *'TANTRUM'*
'C' GROUP: (NONE)

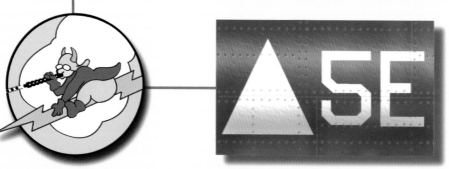

384ᵀᴴ FIGHTER SQDN.
•CALL SIGNS•
'A' GROUP: *'GOLDFISH'*
'B' GROUP: *'ZEETA'*
'C' GROUP: (NONE)

385ᵀᴴ FIGHTER SQDN.
•CALL SIGNS•
'A' GROUP: *'EGGFLIP'*
'B' GROUP: *'PILLOW'*
'C' GROUP: (NONE)

364TH FIGHTER GROUP

ASSIGNED 8TH AAF/FEB-44
STATION NO. 375
HONINGTON A/F, SUFFOIK
C.10-FEB-44 THRU C.3-NOV-45
STATION CALL SIGN:
'OUTSIDE'

CAMPAIGNS
• AIR OFFENSIVE-EUROPE • NORMANDY •
• NORTHERN FRANCE • RHINELAND •
• ARDENNES-ALSACE • CENTRAL EUROPE •

The 364thFG adopted the practice of applying the last three digits of the aircraft tail number to both sides of the nacelle nose. These numbers were normally eight to ten inches in height, painted yellow with most stencil lines remaining open.

An additional adaptation of the 364th was the 'Droop Snoot' (see #737 above) on many of its P-38s beginning in April 1944.

One thing the 364thFG did not adopt, even after converting to the P-51 Mustang, was the use of squadron colors. Instead the use of geometric symbols was incorporated as identifying squadron markers. As a general rule these devices measured 30 inches at their widest point, the 385thFS triangle was equilateral in configuration. Tail numbers were either masked out prior to marker application or reinstated over these symbols with either yellow or black paint. Individual aircraft call letters were relocated to the inner surface fin areas, using white paint, and measuring approximately 30in. in height

The 364th was the last AAF fighter group to join the 8thAAF, entering combat with venerable P-38J in early March 1944. As was the custom with other Lightning units within the Eighth, the squadrons of the 364thFG adopted the practice of recording individual mission tally scores on the port side of the nacelle, just forward and below the cockpit windscreen.

These individual symbols were applied with either yellow or white paint

The 364thFG continued to use white as the basis of their Group color nose markings. As an additional distinguishing feature, six-inch tall medium blue color bars were incorporated within the twelve-inch white nose section encompassing the forward area of the engine cowling. These bars corresponded to the horizontal axis of the fuselage and fully encircled the cowling.

364TH FIGHTER GROUP
LOCKHEED P-38 'LIGHTNING'
C. FEB'44–JUL'44

Most combat aircraft assigned to the 364thFtrGrp received a Droop-Snoot treatment in addition to the duplication, usually in yellow, of the last three digits of the aircraft's tail number. These numbers were located on the forward center section of the nacelle, just aft the white vertical Droop-Snoot stripe.

The 364thFtrGrp adopted the use of geometric symbols as squadron markers verses a more typical color coding system. Specifications called for these markers to measure 30in. at the widest point. With the application of these geometric squadron symbols the existing tail numbers were handled in one of two ways: The entire number was either block-masked out, leaving an unpainted horizontal strip or reinstated in either black or yellow paint over the newly applied squadron symbol.

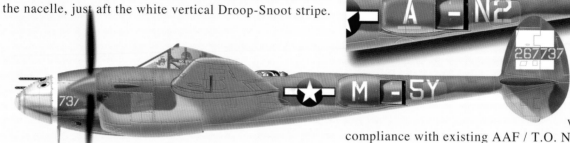

In March 1944 the 364thFG adopted the use of white spinners as its unit marker. The leading twelve inches of each engine cowling were similarly painted white for enhanced visibility.

All fuselage codes were applied with white paint in full compliance with existing AAF / T.O. No.07-1-1 (revised). Individual call letters were relocated to the inner fin areas and the radiator housings. A bar symbol was sometimes applied to the vent door separating the call letter and squadron code. A thin horizontal bar located beneath the call letter indicated a Second-in-Squadron aircraft inventory status.

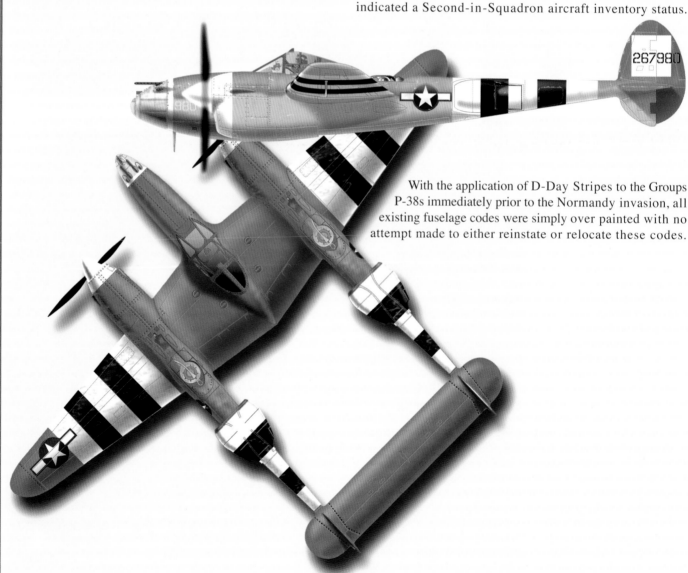

With the application of D-Day Stripes to the Groups P-38s immediately prior to the Normandy invasion, all existing fuselage codes were simply over painted with no attempt made to either reinstate or relocate these codes.

NORTH AMERICAN P-51 'MUSTANG'
c. JUL'44 / VE-DAY

- **383rd Squadron**: Varied between 28-40 inches in diameter with call letters between 18- 30 inches accordingly.
- **384th Squadron**: Approximately 24 inches square containing an 18 inch call letter.
- **385th Squadron**: Consisted of an 28 inch base line with 36 inch diagonal sides and a 24 inch tall call letter.

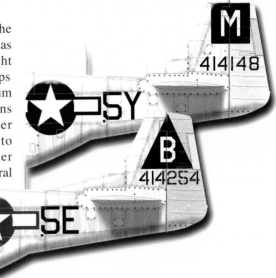

With the 364th Fighter Groups transition to the Mustang the existing geographic symbols were adopted for continued use as official squadron markers. There were however some slight modifications to these symbols when applied to the Groups P-51s. Whereas the squadrons had utilized a 30in. maximum measure on their respective applications, the actual dimensions as applied to the Mustang were varied. The 384th Fighter Squadron significantly reduced the overall size of its square to accommodate the existing tail numbers. The 385th Fighter Squadrons original marker was transformed from an equilateral to an isosceles triangle giving this symbol a narrower base but maintaining an approximate height equal to the original 30in. The 383rd Fighter Squadrons marker on the other hand varied in diameter from between 28in. to 40in. containing a call letter with a height anywhere from 18in. to 30in. In these larger marker applications the tail number was simply over-painted and no attempt was made to reinstate them.

An interesting characteristic, unique among the 364th Fighter Group, was the 383rd Squadrons policy of applying to its aircraft a squadron code with a height measuring 30in., this as opposed to the other squadrons 18in. to 20in. The reason for these applications is unknown but its use was consistent among virtually all P-51s assigned to the 383rdFS from the beginning.

This battle damage photo serves to illustrate a typical over-painting of the tail number with the application of the 383rd Fighter Squadrons circular marker. Note also the black QIM's on the horizontal stabilizer. These and the companion wing markers continued to be displayed on a good number of 364th Fighter Group Mustangs long after most other groups had abandoned their use. The UK/QIM's had been superceded by the Invasion Stripes in early June of 1944, and in most cases simply not reinstated on USAAF fighter aircraft when the D-Day markers were ultimately removed later that same year. Although not apparent in this photograph, some flight leaders within the 385th Fighter Squadron were known to have utilized decorated trim tabs and/or dorsal fin fillets. The latter consisted of a series of red stripes while the rudder trim tabs were either similarly striped with red and black or painted as a solid red.

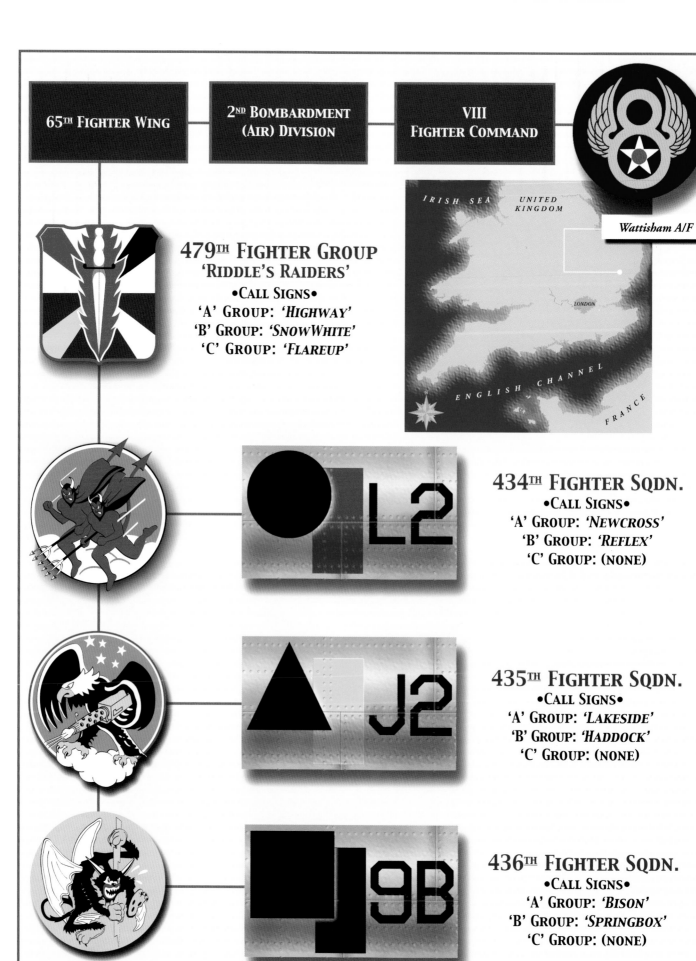

65TH FIGHTER WING | 2ND BOMBARDMENT (AIR) DIVISION | VIII FIGHTER COMMAND

Wattisham A/F

479TH FIGHTER GROUP
'RIDDLE'S RAIDERS'
•CALL SIGNS•
'A' GROUP: *'HIGHWAY'*
'B' GROUP: *'SNOWWHITE'*
'C' GROUP: *'FLAREUP'*

434TH FIGHTER SQDN.
•CALL SIGNS•
'A' GROUP: *'NEWCROSS'*
'B' GROUP: *'REFLEX'*
'C' GROUP: (NONE)

435TH FIGHTER SQDN.
•CALL SIGNS•
'A' GROUP: *'LAKESIDE'*
'B' GROUP: *'HADDOCK'*
'C' GROUP: (NONE)

436TH FIGHTER SQDN.
•CALL SIGNS•
'A' GROUP: *'BISON'*
'B' GROUP: *'SPRINGBOX'*
'C' GROUP: (NONE)

479TH FIGHTER GROUP

ASSIGNED 8TH AAF/APR-44

STATION NO. 377

WATTISHAM A/F, SUFFOIK

C.15-MAY-44 THRU C.23-NOV-45

STATION CALLSIGN:

'HEATER'

CAMPAIGNS
• AIR OFFENSIVE-EUROPE • NORMANDY •
• NORTHERN FRANCE • RHINELAND •
• ARDENNES-ALSACE • CENTRAL EUROPE •

This image is a enlargement of a larger group photograph which contains all of the pilots assigned to the 436th Fighter Squadron in early 1945. Although somewhat grainy, the combat insignia of the 436th can be made out on the left side of three of the pilots leather flight jackets.

The 479th Fighter Groups first combat commander, Lt/Col Kyle L. Riddle, selected the geometric symbols depicted on the facing page to serve as his squadrons' recognition markers. On 10Aug44 Riddle was shot down while flying a mission and was replaced by Col. Hubert A. Zemke, former C.O. of the 56th Fighter Group. Upon assuming command Colonel Zemke immediately directed that colors were to replace the symbols as squadron identifying elements. Col. Zemke was himself shot down several months later and captured by the Germans. Kyle Riddle who had earlier evaded capture, returned to England and subsequently been promoted to full Colonel, once again assumed command of the 479th and retained the new colors.

Upon close examination the photo at left reveals both the official and unofficial insignia of the 434th FtrSqdn adorning the pilots leather flight jacket.

This assemblage of 434th FtrSqdn pilot photos carries the unofficial insignia (depicted in color, lower right) which was adopted after the 479th Fighter Groups conversion to the P-51 Mustang. The original (and official) 'double trouble' image displayed by the 434thFS alluded to the twin boomed configuration of the units original P-38 Lightnings and deemed inappropriate for representing the replacement Mustangs, thus the advent of this newer design.

479TH FIGHTER GROUP
LOCKHEED P-38 'LIGHTNING'
C. MAY-JUL'44

The vast majority of the original allocation of P-38s received by the 479thFG were in natural metal finishes, those delivered with a two-color factory camouflage paint scheme had their respective squadron symbols applied to the outer tail section in white paint as opposed to the black used on the metal finishes. In both cases the standard 30 inch image size was utilized. The call-letter located on the inner tail surfaces were a different matter. These were applied with the same stencils as used on the fuselage codes making these letters 18 inches as opposed to the 30 inch height more commonly used by 8thUSAAF P-38 units.

Immediately prior to the Normandy Invasion, a number of the natural metal finished aircraft received an 'edging' application of a dark green paint to the upper boom and tail surfaces. The top wing and horizontal surface areas were also painted, sometimes in a solid coverage, in other instances with a more typical disruptive pattern. This was no doubt in anticipation of partial deployment of a contingent from the 479thFG to the European continent following the D-Day landings. These paint schemes were phased out by midsummer.

Invasion Stripes were also added to all operational 479thFG Lightnings just prior to D-Day. The fuselage codes were simply over-painted and no attempt was made to reinstate them. It was concluded that the relatively small overall height of these letters (18in.) would have made the codes almost impossible to accurately discern when set against the high contrast of the b&w Invasion Stripes.

LOCKHEED P-38 'LIGHTNING'
C. JUL-SEP'44

Those Lightning's within the 479th Fighter Group bearing a factory applied two-color camouflage paint scheme received the standard P-38 'Droop-Snoot' treatment. In addition to this, all paint was removed from the propeller spinners as well as a 12-18 inch section from the forward area of both engine cowlings.

When squadron colors were ultimately adopted by the 479th Fighter Group there were actually only two; ANA No.619 Bright Red was selected for the 434th Fighter Squadron and ANA No.505 Light Yellow was assigned to the 435th Fighter Squadron. These colors were applied to both rudders and as a rule, the aircraft tail numbers were repainted shortly thereafter. The 436th Fighter Squadron was not originally assigned a color and in fact did not utilize one until the Group converted to the P-51 Mustang in mid-summer of this same year.

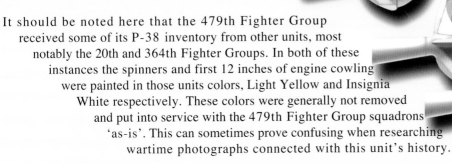

It should be noted here that the 479th Fighter Group received some of its P-38 inventory from other units, most notably the 20th and 364th Fighter Groups. In both of these instances the spinners and first 12 inches of engine cowling were painted in those units colors, Light Yellow and Insignia White respectively. These colors were generally not removed and put into service with the 479th Fighter Group squadrons 'as-is'. This can sometimes prove confusing when researching wartime photographs connected with this unit's history.

Even after complying with SHAEF Operation Memo No. 23 of July 1944 which confined Invasion Stripes to the under surface areas only of U.K. based fighter aircraft, the original 479th Fighter Group fuselage codes were not reinstated on the P-38s.

NORTH AMERICAN P-51 'MUSTANG'
C. SEP'44 / VE-DAY

Upon receipt of their replacement P-51s, squadron colors were immediately applied to the rudder areas. These colors remained unchanged from those assigned to the Groups former P-38s. those being ANA No.619/Bright Red for the 434thFS and ANA No.505/Light Yellow for the 435thFS. The aircraft tail numbers were either removed entirely or simply over painted at this time. D-Day 'half-stripes' were initially applied as per SHAEF instructions but this practice tapered off considerably when word filtered down to the fighter groups of the pending cessation of the use of these devices.

Upon delivery all UK/QIM's were either partially or entirely removed from the nose and empennage areas of the new P-51s. One notable addition to the 479thFtrGrps identity was the introduction of ANA No.515/Gloss Black as the new color for the 436th Fighter Squadron. This unit originally adopted a checkerboard pattern consisting of a series of 12 inch squares applied to their aircraft's rudders. The serial numbers were completely removed from all tail sections with this application. Use of this pattern was discontinued however the following November in favor of a solid paint coverage of the entire rudder surface area. Later handling of tail numbers among the squadrons of the 479thFG ran the full gambit of applications and varied from complete removal, over painting, block-masking to full reinstatement. In the latter case the 434th and 435th Fighter Squadrons used either black, yellow or in a few cases, a combination of the two when reapplying numbers over the newly painted rudders. The use of a bar positioned under a call letter was adopted to denote a Second-in-Squadron status.

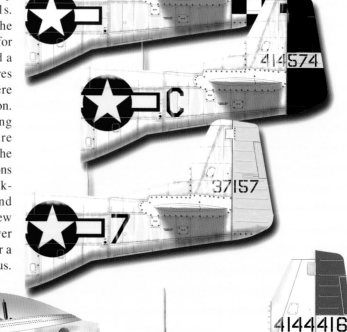

8TH/USAAF
SCOUTING FORCE

The concept for the creation of a small advance aerial force to precede 8thAAF bomber formations on their missions was the brain child of Army Air Force Colonel Budd J. Peaslee, or 'Uncle Budd' as he was affectionately referred to by his subordinates. Peaslee was all to familiar with the many problems encountered by VIII Bomber Command on any given mission having commanded the 384th Bomb Group from 18Dec42 until 6Sep43. As a result of this hands-on experience Col. Peaslee lined up all his ducks and submitted a formal proposal for the formation of a Scouting Force to the Commanding Officer/8thAAF, Brigadier General James 'Jimmy' Doolittle. Always a man of vision where his beloved Air Corps was concerned, Gen. Doolittle approved Peaslee's plan and ordered the formation of Scouting Force (Experimental) for immediate trial and evaluation and Col. Peaslee was appointed by Doolittle to head up the newly formed unit.

As Peaslee envisioned it the primary duty of the aerial scouts would be to proceed each bomber stream and evaluate existing weather conditions over the missions primary, and if

COL.BUDD PEASLEE/384THBG

necessary, alternate target areas. The Scouts would then communicate this information to the Mission Commanders thus resulting in decreased mission duration, increased effectiveness and, more importantly, a reduction in the per mission casualty rate.

Secondary duties for the Scouts would be to assist the bomb groups at their respective assembly points with pre-strike form-ups and than help maintain a tight box formation once the bombers were enroute to their target. Eventually, the Scouts would also prove to be an effective asset in assisting the assigned fighter escort with fending off enemy aerial attacks. This however would come only after some of the units pilots gained enough fighter time to enable them to go head-to-head with the vaunted Luftwaffe.

But in June of 1944 all of this was somewhere off in the future if indeed the Scouts were to have a future at all beyond this crucial experimental phase.

Colonel Peaslee's first order of business was to recruit eight volunteer bomber pilots. A prerequisite for consideration to a posting to the Scouts was completion of one full combat tour within the ETO in heavy bombers. Rounding out the Scouts starting lineup required an additional eight experienced fighter pilots. Both the pilots and twelve P-51D's Mustangs (including the necessary maintenance crews) were supplied by the 355th Fighter Group at Steeple Morden Air Field. The Scouts were attached to the 355thFG for logistical support and as a training ground for the former bomber pilots. Because of their first hand experience with bombing missions, the ex-bomber pilots turned Scouts would assume tactical control of each sortie. However until such a time as these men became familiar with their new aircraft and well versed in current aerial combat tactics, actual encounters with the Luftwaffe would be handled by the seasoned fighter pilots.

Eventually many of the former 'Heavy Drivers' would themselves become accomplished fighter jocks, but in the meantime this system of rotating responsibilities would prove highly effective and undoubtedly saved many a young airmen's life.

The newly formed Scouts adopted a duel set of call signs to identify themselves. 'Borax' was an existing call-sign currently in use by the 355th Fighter Group and this was selected to designate the fighter pilot contingent of the new unit. The former bomber pilots adopted 'Buckeye' as their respective call sign.

Deciding on visual means of differentiating the Scouts from other elements of the 355th Fighter Group became the next order of business. The Groups identifying color was white with the 354th, 357th and 358th Fighter Squadrons individual colors being red, blue and yellow respectively. These colors were applied as a twelve inch band on the leading edge of the engine cowling in addition to the entire rudder area of each squadrons P-51D Mustangs. As the Scouts would be flying the same type of aircraft and it was decided to adopt a twelve inch white engine cowling band as the unit marker. This was reminiscent of the original QIM markings of the 355th Fighter Groups original P-51's. It was further decided that the rudder area of the Scouts Mustangs would remain unpainted, perhaps in an effort to keep from drawing undo attention from enemy ground observers. In place of a rudder color the Scouts chose to apply a black bar *under* their aircrafts fuselage code. These codes corresponded with that of the particular squadron a given Scout was assigned, i.e. 'WR'-354thFS, 'OS'-357thFS and 'YF'-358thFS. These fuselage code bars and the twelve inch white engine cowling would be the only distinguishing markers displayed by the Scouts during the remainder of their trial evaluation phase at Steeple Morden Air Field.

It didn't take the newly formed unit long to 'train-up' and the scouts flew their first bomber mission in July 1944. The effectiveness of the Scout concept became immediately apparent and General Doolittle, never a man to be accused of indecisiveness, ordered the formation of three Scouting Forces after only the fifth mission completed by the SF(X) unit. Each of the three Bombardment (later Air) Divisions within the VIII AAF structure was to have a Scouting Force attached to it.

The 1st Scouting Force would be stationed at Honington and later at Bassingbourn Air Fields under the command of Col. Budd Peaslee. The 2nd SF would be headed up by Lt. Col. John A. Brooks III and based at Steeple Morden. The 3rdSF was to be under the leadership of Lt.Col. Vincent W. Masters and this unit would call Wormingford Air Field its home. All three of the Scouting Force units began operations by the end of summer 1944 and would continue to serve the 8thAAF with distinction until wars end.

As for the original Scouting Force (Experimental) it flew its thirty-fifth and final combat mission September 12th 1944 having more than succeeded in proving the merit of an advance weather recon force for the 'Heavy's'.

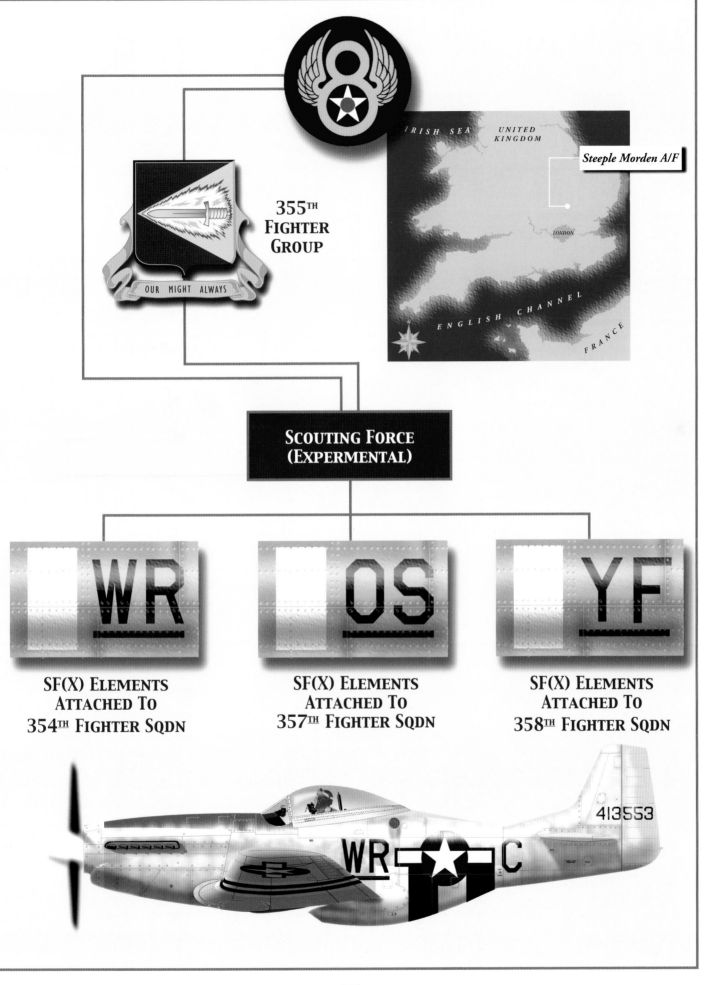

355TH
FIGHTER
GROUP

OUR MIGHT ALWAYS

IRISH SEA · UNITED KINGDOM

Steeple Morden A/F

LONDON

ENGLISH CHANNEL

FRANCE

N

SCOUTING FORCE
(EXPERMENTAL)

WR

OS

YF

SF(X) ELEMENTS
ATTACHED TO
354TH FIGHTER SQDN

SF(X) ELEMENTS
ATTACHED TO
357TH FIGHTER SQDN

SF(X) ELEMENTS
ATTACHED TO
358TH FIGHTER SQDN

WR ★ C

413553

67TH FIGHTER WING

1ST BOMBARDMENT (AIR) DIVISION

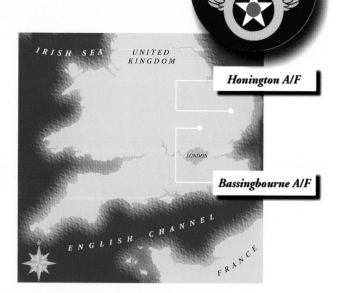

Honington A/F

Bassingbourne A/F

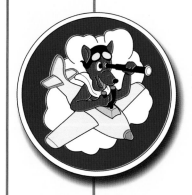

1ST SCOUTING FORCE
•CALL SIGN•
'CAVALRY'

1ST S/F ELEMENTS ATTACHED TO 383RD FIGHT⟶ER SQDN.
•CALL SIGN•
(UNKNOWN)

1ST S/F ELEMENTS ATTACHED TO 384TH FIGHTER SQDN.
•CALL SIGN•
(UNKNOWN)

1ST S/F ELEMENTS ATTACHED TO 385TH FIGHTER SQDN.
•CALL SIGN•
(UNKNOWN)

ASSIGNED 8TH AAF/19SEP44
1.) STATION NO. 375
HONINGTON A/F SUFFOLK: (THRU MAR'45)
STATION CALL SIGN: 'OUTSIDE'

2.) STATION NO. 121
BASSINGBOURN A/F CAMBRIDGESHIRE:
(UNTIL V-E DAY)
STATION CALL SIGN: 'FRONTPIECE'

The 1st S/F was attached to the 364th Fighter Group for logistical support at the beginning of September 1944 and would complete one hundred and seven scouting missions from this base before transferring to Bassingbourn Air Field.

The black UK/QIM's were removed from the tail area of all P-51's just as they had been from all 364th Fighter Group Mustangs. This was done in order to make room for the individual 18-30 inch tall aircraft call-letter which was applied with black paint. Unlike the 364thFG no squadron symbols were incorporated as part of the Scouts tail marking. The Scouts did however adopt the respective squadron codes to which each aircraft was assigned and, in keeping with Group policy, these were located aft the national insignia on both sides of the fuselage.

364TH FIGHTER GROUP

1ST SCOUTING FORCE

Equipped with the same natural metal finished P-51D Mustang as the 364thFG, the Scouts selected as their marking a red spinner combined with a 12in white engine cowling. As an additional identifying element the Scouts applied a red trim to the vertical stabilizer edge beginning at the forward dorsal fin fillet and terminating at, or near, the lower rudder area. The outside edges of the horizontal stabilizers received a similar treatment that would sometimes fully encompass front, side and back edges. Other applications terminated at a point intersecting the elevator on the outside edge of the horizontal stabilizer as depicted in the adjacent illustration.

The 1stSF transferred to Bassingbourn A/F, home of the 91st Bomb Group on 10Mar45 and was subsequently re-designated the 857th Bomb Squadron. The original 857thBS had been assigned to the 492nd Bomb Group, which had been disbanded on 11Aug44 (Refer to page 121, Battle Colors/Vol.I). The reconstituted 857th BS were to retain the original '9H' squadron code that had been issued to its predecessor and this was to replace the 364thFG fuselage codes. The 857thBS continued to fly their P-51 Mustangs and retained the original nose and empennage markings. A total of twenty-four weather reconnaissance/bombing missions were flown from Bassingbourn A/F, the last of which occurred on 25Apr45.

65ᴺᵀᴴ FIGHTER WING

2ᴺᴰ BOMBARDMENT (AIR) DIVISION

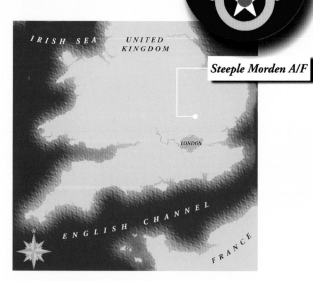

Steeple Morden A/F

2ᴺᴰ SCOUTING FORCE
•CALL SIGN•
''BOOTLEG'

2ᴺᴰ S/F ELEMENTS ATTACHED TO 354ᵀᴴ FIGHTER SQDN.
•CALL SIGN•
(UNKNOWN)

2ᴺᴰ S/F ELEMENTS ATTACHED TO 357ᵀᴴ FIGHTER SQDN.
•CALL SIGN•
(UNKNOWN)

2ᴺᴰ S/F ELEMENTS ATTACHED TO 358ᵀᴴ FIGHTER SQDN.
•CALL SIGN•
(UNKNOWN)

ASSIGNED 8TH AAF/25AUG44
STATION NO. 122
STEEPLE MORDEN A/F,
CAMBRIDGESHIRE
STATION CALL SIGN:
'TOWROPE'
UNTIL APRIL '45, THEREAFTER
'TOOL ROOM'

355TH
FIGHTER GROUP

OUR MIGHT ALWAYS

There are unfortunately very few distinguishing characteristics associated with the 2nd Scouting Force. The 2ndSF retained the white spinner and matching twelve-inch engine cowling originally utilized by Scouting Force (Experimental) but did not adopt any additional unit identification color marker.

The 2ndSF took up residence at Steeple Morden replacing the recently disbanded Scouting Force (Experimental). Whereas SF(X) had located a bar *under* their aircrafts fuselage codes as an identifying marker, the recently constituted 2nd Scouting Force elected to reposition this very same element *above* the codes. The codes themselves remained unchanged and were the same 355thFG squadron codes used by the new units predecessor, Scouting Force (Experimental).

The U.K./QIM's were apparently removed almost immediately from the entire empennage area of virtually all-2nd Scouting Force Mustangs shortly after this units activation. At the time of this writing there was no evidence to indicate that the 2ndSF even bothered to apply the post D-Day' modified' Invasion Stripes to any of their aircraft. The wing QIM's do appear in some photos but these markers also disappeared in short order. Other photographs of the period indicate that at least some of the Scouting Force elements attached to the 357th Fighter Squadron may have applied that squadrons blue color to their trim tabs but confirmation on this is as yet still pending.

66TH FIGHTER WING

3RD BOMBARDMENT (AIR) DIVISION

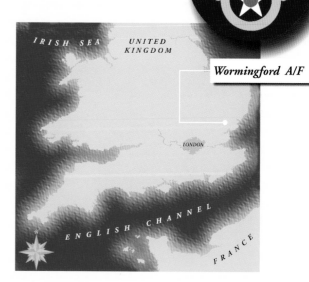

IRISH SEA

UNITED KINGDOM

Wormingford A/F

LONDON

ENGLISH CHANNEL

FRANCE

3RD SCOUTING FORCE
•CALL SIGN•
'KODAK'

3RD S/F ELEMENTS ATTACHED TO 38TH FIGHTER SQDN.
•CALL SIGN•
(UNKNOWN)

3RD S/F ELEMENTS ATTACHED TO 338TH FIGHTER SQDN.
•CALL SIGN•
(UNKNOWN)

3RD S/F ELEMENTS ATTACHED TO 343RD FIGHTER SQDN.
•CALL SIGN•
(UNKNOWN)

55TH FIGHTER GROUP

PURSUIT TO DEFEND

Upon activation the 3rd Scouting Force was attached to the 55th Fighter Group, which supplied the Force with logistical support. The 3rd Scouts would adopt several of the identifying characteristics of the 55thFG in addition to applying unique marking variations of their own to their P-51D Mustangs.

Unlike the 1st and 2nd Scouting Forces, the 3rdSF readily adopted the entire nose markings of the fighter group to which it was attached. It chose instead to differentiate itself from the 55th Fighter Group aircraft by means of a distinct tail marking. The distinctive rudder markings adopted by the 3rd Scouting Force consisted of a checkerboard pattern consisting of a series of alternating red and white six-inch squares. The tail number was reinstated over this pattern. In addition to this colorful marking a red stripe was applied to the leading edge of the tail emanating at the dorsal fin fillet and terminating at the junction point with the rudder. Initially the existing tail QIM marking stripe was simply over painted.

The 3rd Scouting Force adopted the fuselage codes of the 55th Fighter Groups 38th, 338th and 343rd Fighter Squadrons. These codes were of the same standard size and location as employed by these squadrons and like their counterparts, the 3rdSF was extremely lax when it came to filling in the stencil lines on both fuselage codes as well as re-applied tail numbers.

As their inventory of Mustangs increased the 3rd Scouting Force employed the use of a black horizontal bar positioned immediately under an aircrafts fuselage call-letter in order to denote a second issuance of that letter within the 3rdSF.

On 17Feb45 the 3rd Scouting Force was consolidated with the 862nd Bomb Squadron, which had been recently assigned to Wormingford A/F. Equipped with B-17's, the 862nd would fly weather reconnaissance missions over and around the channel area. This unit adopted the checkerboard rudder pattern of the 3rd Scouting Force but supplemented red and white with the green and yellow colors used on 55th Fighter Group on nose markings. The 3rdSF would continue to fly their Mustangs with no change to their existing aircraft markings. The original bomber escort/recon assignment of the 3rdSF also remained unchanged and a total of 140 such missions were carried out from Wormingford, the last being conducted on 21Apr45.

Within the annals of military history it is an unfortunate fact that small, highly specialized units are all to often overlooked by post war historians focusing on the 'big picture'. Such was the fate of the 8thAAF Scouting Force. Despite the enormous contribution made by these small units they were virtually ignored in the annals of the European Air War. Fortunately, from time to time an individual will come along who possesses the determination to correct these oversights and in the case of the Scouting Force that individual was a man by the name of Dick Atkins, himself an AAF/USAF veteran. It took Atkins over a decade to unravel the complete history of the Scouts, but the end result was well worth the effort. The Historical Branch of the United States Air Force is now revising its records to reflect the combat history and contributions made by this elite force.

As brief as the Scouts involvement may have been when compared with other units serving in the ETO they nevertheless lost a total of twenty four of their pilots while at the same time racking-up twenty two victories against the Luftwaffe, and this in spite of the fact that the mission of the Scouts was not to function as a fighter unit. The insignia at left is of post war origin, very post war in fact. The formation of the Scouting Force Association is a rather recent development and one of the goals set by Scouts researcher Dick Atkins of bringing together veterans, their descendants and supporters into a fraternal organization. For those interested in a detailed study of these units the following publication is recommended: *'Fighting Scouts of the Eighth Air Force /1944-1945'* by E. Richard Atkins, 1996. This book is currently out of print but copies may still be obtained through various sources.

8TH/USAAF RECONNAISSANCE UNITS

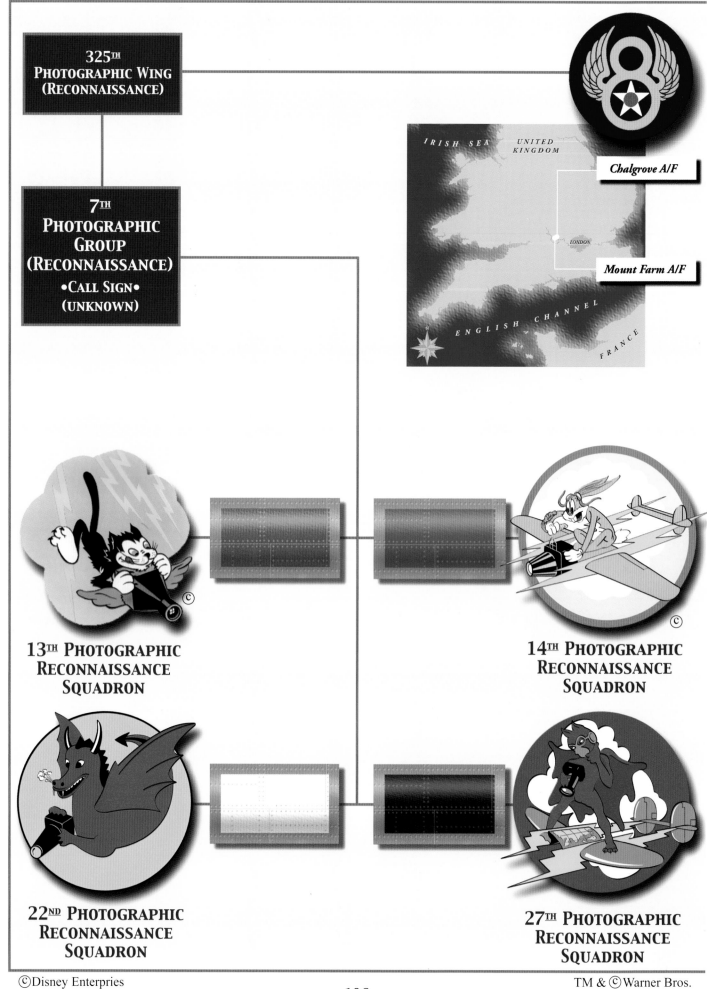

325TH PHOTOGRAPHIC WING (RECONNAISSANCE)

7TH PHOTOGRAPHIC GROUP (RECONNAISSANCE)
•CALL SIGN•
(UNKNOWN)

IRISH SEA

UNITED KINGDOM

Chalgrove A/F

LONDON

Mount Farm A/F

ENGLISH CHANNEL

FRANCE

13TH PHOTOGRAPHIC RECONNAISSANCE SQUADRON

14TH PHOTOGRAPHIC RECONNAISSANCE SQUADRON

22ND PHOTOGRAPHIC RECONNAISSANCE SQUADRON

27TH PHOTOGRAPHIC RECONNAISSANCE SQUADRON

7th PHOTOGRAPHIC GROUP (RECONNAISSANCE)

ASSIGNED 8TH AAF/7-JUL-43
1.) STATION NO.234
MOUNT FARM A/F, OXFORDSHIRE
CALL SIGN 'SKATERINK'
C.7-JUL-43 THRU C.22-MAR-45
2.) STATION NO.465
CHALGROVE A/F, OXFORDSHIRE
CALL SIGN 'BUZZSAW'
C.22-MAR-45 THRU V-E DAY

CAMPAIGNS

- AIR OFFENSIVE-EUROPE •
- AIR OFFENSIVE, EUROPE • TUNISIA •
- NORMANDY • NORTHERN FRANCE •
- RHINELAND • ARDENNES-ALSACE •
- CENTRAL EUROPE •

The 13th Photographic Reconnaissance Squadron actually arrived in England a good seven months earlier than the 7th Photographic Group (R) The 13th was originally posted to Podingham Air Field on 2 Dec 42 where it was attached to the 8th AAF for duty with the 1st Bombardment Wing. The 22nd Photographic Reconnaissance Squadron was temporarily assigned to the 5th Photographic Reconnaissance and Mapping Group prior to that unit's reassignment to the 12th AAF the following summer. With the arrival of the 7th Photographic Group (Reconnaissance) in Great Britain, both squadrons were subsequently transferred to that unit on July 7, 1943.

If SD-110 Codes were assigned to the squadrons of the 7thPG(R), they did not appear on any of the Groups aircraft during the course of the war. Given the nature of this units operations, this ommission was most certainly done for security reasons. At the end of hostilities however the squadrons were assigned standard 'anti-buzzing' codes, which were displayed on the undersurface of the left wing of all operational aircraft. These codes were as follows; 'ES'-13thPS, 'QU'-14thPS and 'G2'-27thPS. The code for the 22ndPS is unknown at this time.

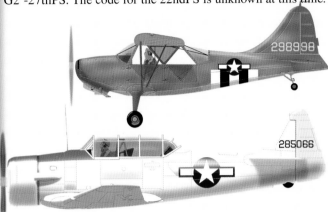

Additional aircraft flown by the 7th Photographic Group (R) included an L-5 Stinson 'Sentinel', a single AT-6D North American 'Texan' and a AT-23B (B-26) Martin 'Marauder' (not shown). The most interesting auxiliary aircraft of the 7thPG(R) was perhaps the B-25C Mitchell Medium Bomber assigned to the unit, which incidently was the single ship of its type within the entire inventory of the 8th AAF. Originally delivered to the Group adorned with a standard factory applied two-color camouflage paint scheme. This was quickly removed and supplemented with an overall application of RAF/PRU Blue. In addition to communications duty this ship was utilized for nighttime photographic reconnaissance missions along the French coastline prior to the D-Day landings. In the final months just prior to V-E Day all surface paint was stripped from this aircraft and she finished out the war in an all-natural metal finished state.

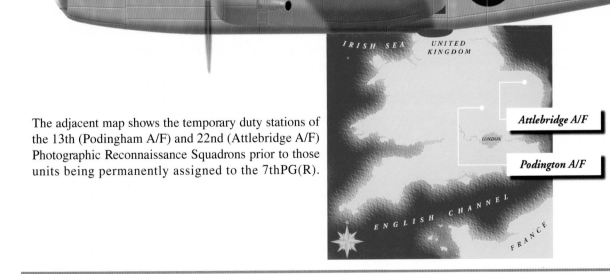

The adjacent map shows the temporary duty stations of the 13th (Podingham A/F) and 22nd (Attlebridge A/F) Photographic Reconnaissance Squadrons prior to those units being permanently assigned to the 7thPG(R).

IRISH SEA UNITED KINGDOM

LONDON

Attlebridge A/F

Podington A/F

ENGLISH CHANNEL

FRANCE

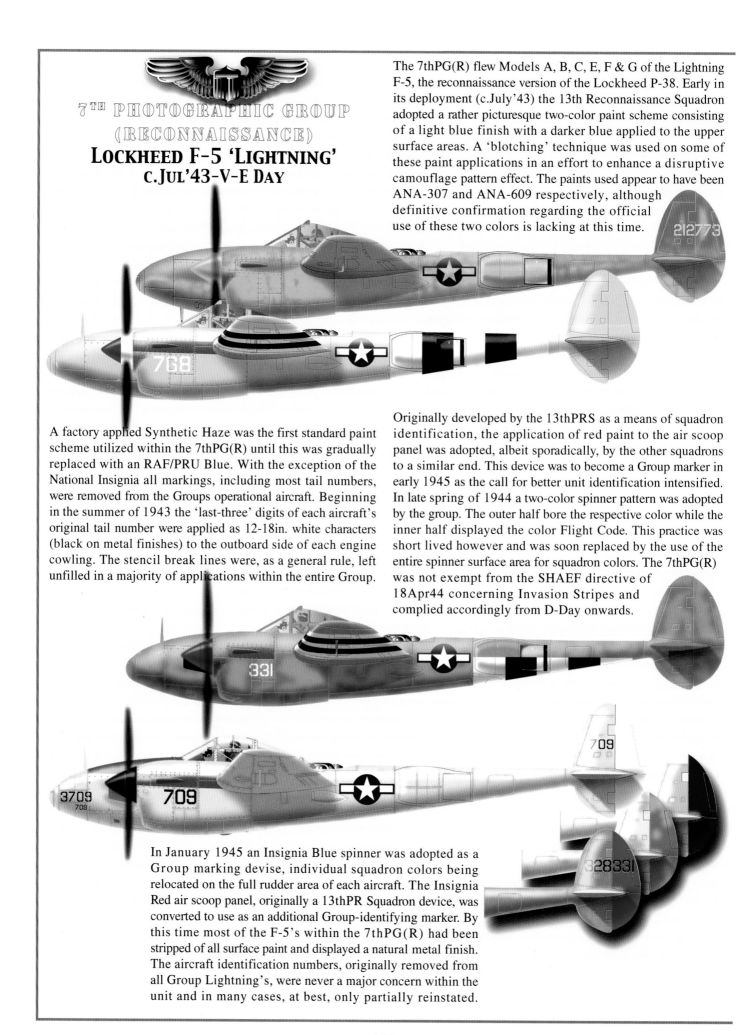

7ᵀᴴ PHOTOGRAPHIC GROUP (RECONNAISSANCE)
LOCKHEED F-5 'LIGHTNING'
C.JUL'43-V-E DAY

The 7thPG(R) flew Models A, B, C, E, F & G of the Lightning F-5, the reconnaissance version of the Lockheed P-38. Early in its deployment (c.July'43) the 13th Reconnaissance Squadron adopted a rather picturesque two-color paint scheme consisting of a light blue finish with a darker blue applied to the upper surface areas. A 'blotching' technique was used on some of these paint applications in an effort to enhance a disruptive camouflage pattern effect. The paints used appear to have been ANA-307 and ANA-609 respectively, although definitive confirmation regarding the official use of these two colors is lacking at this time.

A factory applied Synthetic Haze was the first standard paint scheme utilized within the 7thPG(R) until this was gradually replaced with an RAF/PRU Blue. With the exception of the National Insignia all markings, including most tail numbers, were removed from the Groups operational aircraft. Beginning in the summer of 1943 the 'last-three' digits of each aircraft's original tail number were applied as 12-18in. white characters (black on metal finishes) to the outboard side of each engine cowling. The stencil break lines were, as a general rule, left unfilled in a majority of applications within the entire Group.

Originally developed by the 13thPRS as a means of squadron identification, the application of red paint to the air scoop panel was adopted, albeit sporadically, by the other squadrons to a similar end. This device was to become a Group marker in early 1945 as the call for better unit identification intensified. In late spring of 1944 a two-color spinner pattern was adopted by the group. The outer half bore the respective color while the inner half displayed the color Flight Code. This practice was short lived however and was soon replaced by the use of the entire spinner surface area for squadron colors. The 7thPG(R) was not exempt from the SHAEF directive of 18Apr44 concerning Invasion Stripes and complied accordingly from D-Day onwards.

In January 1945 an Insignia Blue spinner was adopted as a Group marking devise, individual squadron colors being relocated on the full rudder area of each aircraft. The Insignia Red air scoop panel, originally a 13thPR Squadron device, was converted to use as an additional Group-identifying marker. By this time most of the F-5's within the 7thPG(R) had been stripped of all surface paint and displayed a natural metal finish. The aircraft identification numbers, originally removed from all Group Lightning's, were never a major concern within the unit and in many cases, at best, only partially reinstated.

7ᵀᴴ PHOTOGRAPHIC GROUP (RECONNAISSANCE)
'SPITFIRE' MK. XI
c.OCT'43–APR'45

Throughout their entire length of service with the 7thPG(R), the Spits' bore an overall RAF/PRU Blue color scheme. In numerous cases where the existing RAF insignia was not removed, the application of the USAAF Type-4 National Insignia was somewhat larger than normal when this devise needed to over paint the existing 32in. RAF fuselage roundel.

Beginning in the spring of 1944 propeller spinners were painted a solid color in accordance with each aircraft's respective Flight assignment. At this same time the original four-inch tall Sky Blue fuselage codes were duplicated in white paint on the tails of all the Groups Spitfires.

These new letters were approximately six inches in height with the numerals measuring in at around twelve inches. As with the Groups F-5's, the Spitfires were not exempt from the SHAEF memo of 18Apr44 regarding the application of Distinctive Markings-Aircraft and thus, beginning 5Jun44, all 7thPG(R) Mk.XI's would display the proper D-Day Invasion Stripes.

In January 1944 all 7thPG(R) Mk.XI Spitfires were consolidated within the 14th Photo Reconnaissance Squadron. In January of the following year these adopted the Groups blue spinner and red exhaust panels in addition to the medium green tail rudder of the 14thPRS.

7ᵀᴴ PHOTOGRAPHIC GROUP (RECONNAISSANCE)
NORTH AMERICAN P-51 'MUSTANG'
c.JAN'45–V-E DAY

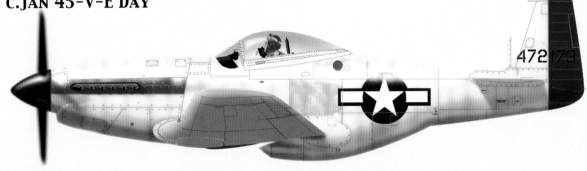

The P-51 was a late arrival to the 7thPG(R) and only two models, the D and K Series, saw service with this unit. Serving as fighter escorts for the Groups unarmed photo reconnaissance ships, the Mustangs adopted the standardized Group spinner and cowling markers along with respective squadron markings.

As with the F-5's, no SD-110 fuselage codes were applied to these aircraft. At wars end however both the Groups P-51's and F-5's would display black post war 'anti-buzz' markings on the underside of the left wing. The units Spitfires were returned to the RAF in May'45 and thus not subjected to these markings.

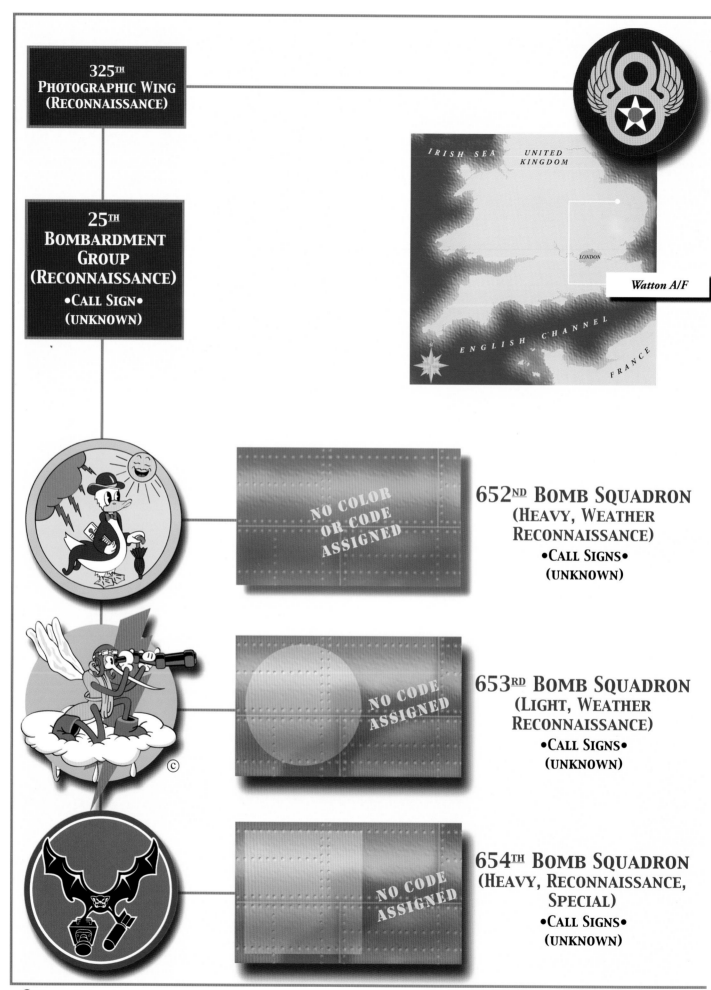

325TH PHOTOGRAPHIC WING (RECONNAISSANCE)

25TH BOMBARDMENT GROUP (RECONNAISSANCE)
•CALL SIGN•
(UNKNOWN)

Watton A/F

IRISH SEA UNITED KINGDOM

LONDON

ENGLISH CHANNEL

FRANCE

NO COLOR OR CODE ASSIGNED

652ND BOMB SQUADRON (HEAVY, WEATHER RECONNAISSANCE)
•CALL SIGNS•
(UNKNOWN)

NO CODE ASSIGNED

653RD BOMB SQUADRON (LIGHT, WEATHER RECONNAISSANCE)
•CALL SIGNS•
(UNKNOWN)

NO CODE ASSIGNED

654TH BOMB SQUADRON (HEAVY, RECONNAISSANCE, SPECIAL)
•CALL SIGNS•
(UNKNOWN)

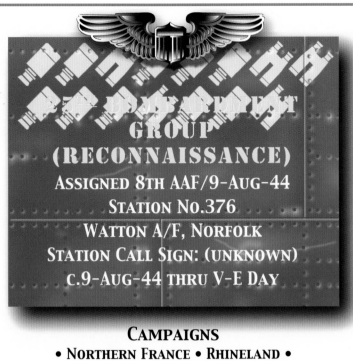

25TH BOMBARDMENT GROUP (RECONNAISSANCE)

ASSIGNED 8TH AAF/9-AUG-44
STATION No.376
WATTON A/F, NORFOLK
STATION CALL SIGN: (UNKNOWN)
c.9-AUG-44 THRU V-E DAY

CAMPAIGNS
• NORTHERN FRANCE • RHINELAND •
• ARDENNES-ALSACE • CENTRAL EUROPE •

Originally formed at Watton A/F as the 802nd Reconnaissance Group (Provisional) on 22Apr44, this unit underwent a period of training, specifically involving the de Havilland Mosquito which had been supplied by the British Air Ministry. On 9Aug44 the 802ndRG(P) was reconstituted as the 25th Bombardment Group (R) and declared fully operational. It might be stretching things a bit to say that at one time or another the 25thBG flew just about everything in the Army Air Force inventory, but in reality such a statement wouldn't be too far off the mark. This units aircraft roster even included a B-25 Mitchell Medium Bomber which was reportedly painted entirely gloss black, however documentation as to the actual application of black on this particular aircraft was unavailable at the time of this writing. In the early stages of the Second World War specialized aerial reconnaissance was, in large part, still in its developmental stages. Along with experimenting with newly developed equipment, determining the best aircraft suited to a particular job was pretty much of a trial-and-error proposition. As the war progressed the 25th Bomb Groups operations became more refined and its use of aircraft became much more selective. As far as colors and markings are concerned however, the unit presented a pretty lackluster image, which was of course necessitated by the need for security due to the nature of the 25thBG's operations.

STINSON L-5

MITCHELL B-25

CONSOLDIATED B-24

BOEING B-17

MARTIN B-26

The 652nd Bomb Squadron (H) conducted long-range weather reconnaissance missions over the Atlantic. Operating with both B-17's and B-24's, these aircraft originally carried a standard two-color camouflage paint scheme but were eventually flown with a natural metal finish towards wars end. A 24in (yellow on paint, black on metal) call letter positioned on the vertical stabilizer just below the identification number were the only identifying marks ever displayed on these aircraft. The original B-25's flown briefly by the 654th BG(S) in early 1944 lacked even a simple call-letter and several of these aircraft had the

serial number on the tail surface painted over in an attempt to maximize security. The B-26's operated by this squadron did adopt for a time an Olive Drab over an ANA-622 Jet (ANA Bulletin No.157, 28Sep43) camouflage pattern developed for night recon operations. Other than this however, the only other distinguishing characteristics consisted of an 18in. yellow call-letter painted on the tail surface just below the aircraft serial number. The small L-5's would, at different times, alternate between displaying the call-letter/serial number combination to showing nothing but the UAAF Type-4 National Insignia.

DE HAVILLAND PR XVI 'MOSQUITO'
C.AUG'44–V–E DAY

The earliest Mosquito's assigned to the Group retained their original RAF Roundel Blue spinners. These would however eventually all be repainted overall with RAF PRU Blue.

The operation of this aircraft within the 25thBG(R) was confined to the 653rd and 654th Squadrons and markings differed according to both time frame as well as usage. The normal operating color was a standard PRU (Photo Recon Unit) Blue utilized by the RAF. The original distinguishing characteristic on these Mosquito's was the application to the lower forward tail section of a white 18in. tall call letter within a 3in. to 4in. thick circular surround. These devices however were short lived due to an ever- increasing number of 'friendly fire' incidents, which pointed out the need for a greatly increased factor of aircraft recognition.

The solution settled upon was the painting of the entire emphannage section with Insignia Red. Prior to painting the tail, a 24in. diameter circle or 24in. square were used to 'block-mask' over the previously applied call letters thus allowing the existing call letter to stand alone after painting. The circle and square elements were adopted by the 653rd and 654th BG's respectively. This practice was later modified, the geometric elements were dropped altogether, the white letter being applied directly over the painted red tail surface area. Yet another variation to these markings was adopted by some of the squadrons XVI's in late 1944, and this consisted of reverting back to the original 18in. white call letter affixed to a solid PRU Blue surface.

The Mosquito's of the 25thBG(R) were not exempt from the SHAEF requirement concerning D-Day Invasion Stripes and were in full compliance with same throughout the full term of this directive. The application of the AN-I-9b National Insignia was slightly larger than that called for on normal AAF applications with a 40in. diameter 'circle/star' configuration being applied to both the fuselage and wing surfaces, the insignia 'bars' likewise being enlarged proportionally.

653rdBS PR XVI's as well as those with the 654thBS involved in daylight missions underwent several modifications such as depicted above.

Those Mk.XVI's within the Group flying 'Joker' and 'Red Stocking' night missions received several different paint and marking treatments as well. The 654thBS(HRS) bore the responsibility for a majority of both nocturnal photo recon and covert OSS operations within the 25thBG(R). Originally these aircraft received an overall repainting using a matt black paint. This was ultimately replaced with high gloss ANA 622 Jet. A red tail, serial number and call-letter were frequently used.

In early May of 1945 both of the Mosquito squadrons officially adopted spinner colors as an additional means of unit identification. The 653rdBS(LWR) elected to return to the original Roundel Blue, which was the standard color used by the RAF. The 654th(HRS) selected Insignia Red as their spinner color.

25ᵀᴴ BOMBARDMENT GROUP (RECONNAISSANCE)

LOCKHEED P-38 'LIGHTNING'
C.AUG'44-V-E DAY

Although the Mk XVI Mosquito conducted the majority of photographic reconnaissance missions within the framework of the 654thBS(HRS), numerous models of P-38 Lightning's also saw service in a photo recon role with this unit. There does not appear to have been any hard and fast rules pertaining to either the painting schemes or marking methods employed with these particular aircraft.

An early practice within the unit was to apply an overall coat of RAF PRU Blue over the existing factory applied two-color, Olive Drab / Neutral Grey camouflage paint. Aircraft serial numbers were sometimes replaced with an individual call letter on each outward facing tail surface as opposed to the more commonly used location on or near the radiator housing. With these applications the 'last three' digits of the a/c serial number were affixed to the outward facing surfaces of each engine cowling. Both these and the call-letters were applied using white paint. The national insignia on many of these Lightning's were 'grayed-out' on both booms. As far as can be determined the use of P-38's within the 25thBG structure was limited to the 654thBS. While this was an excellent aircraft the Mosquito was better suited to the task of photo reconnaissance.

The story of the 25th Bombardment Group (Reconnaissance) is unique within the annals of 8thAAF history; there was really no other unit quite like it. The title *Bomb Group* is extremely deceptive and this was perhaps an intentional designation as it would tend to detract from the units real purpose during World War II. The missions carried out by the three squadrons varied from the gathering of crucial weather data over the Atlantic to top secret operations involving solo night flights over Berlin itself. These missions all had colorful code names such as Grey Pea, Mickey, Red Tail, Blue Stocking, Sky Wave, Frantic and other equally intriguing cryptograms. The men manning the aircraft of both the 653rd and 654th Bomb Squadrons were themselves noteworthy. All were volunteer pilots and navigators and most had previously completed the required thirty-five combat missions while serving with other USAAF bomb groups. Some of the volunteers were British serving airmen who had requested transfer to the units from either the RAF or RCAF.

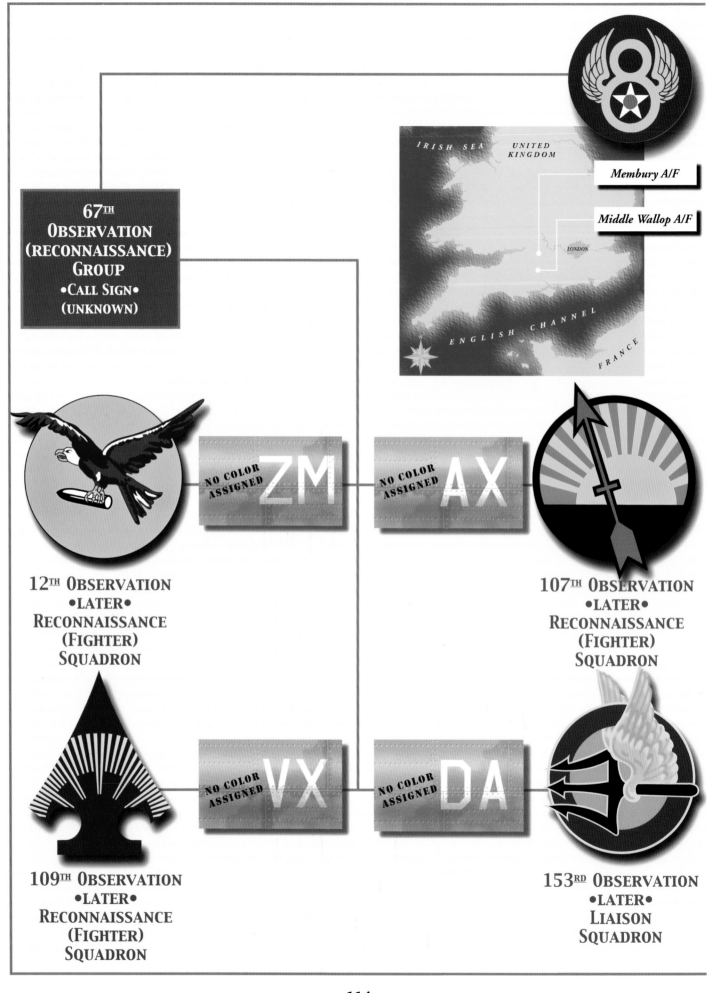

67TH OBSERVATION (RECONNAISSANCE) GROUP
•CALL SIGN•
(UNKNOWN)

Membury A/F

Middle Wallop A/F

IRISH SEA
UNITED KINGDOM
LONDON
ENGLISH CHANNEL
FRANCE

NO COLOR ASSIGNED **ZM**

NO COLOR ASSIGNED **AX**

NO COLOR ASSIGNED **VX**

NO COLOR ASSIGNED **DA**

12TH OBSERVATION
•LATER•
RECONNAISSANCE (FIGHTER) SQUADRON

107TH OBSERVATION
•LATER•
RECONNAISSANCE (FIGHTER) SQUADRON

109TH OBSERVATION
•LATER•
RECONNAISSANCE (FIGHTER) SQUADRON

153RD OBSERVATION
•LATER•
LIAISON SQUADRON

67th OBSERVATION (RECONNAISSANCE) GROUP

ASSIGNED 8TH AAF/AUG-42
1.) STATION NO.466
MEMBURY A/F, BERKSHIRE
c.)SEP-42 THRU c.)OCT-43
STATION CALL SIGN: (UNKNOWN)
*2.) STATION NO.449
MIDDLE WALLOP A/F, HAMPSHIRE
c.DEC-43 THRU c.JUL-44
STATION CALL SIGN: (UNKNOWN)

CAMPAIGNS
•ANTISUBMARINE, AMERICAN THEATER•
• AIR OFFENSIVE-EUROPE •
• NORMANDY • NORTHERN FRANCE •
• RHINELAND • ARDENNES-ALSACE •
• CENTRAL EUROPE •

This unit underwent three changes in official designation from its original formation in August 1941 until V-E Day, ergo the dual Observation/Reconnaissance listing. The 67th was designated as a Reconnaissance Group in May'43, and finally modified to the 67th Tactical Reconnaissance Group (Nov'43).

The 12th Observation Squadron insignia was unofficially adopted by that unit during World War I. When such matters became more formal, the image was formally submitted to the U.S. Army Board of Heraldry following the war and approved by that particular entity on 2Feb24. The 109th Observation Squadrons insignia was officially adopted on 7Mar39. Of the remaining two insignia, those of the 107th and 153rd Observation Squadrons, the only thing that can be said with any certainty is that the images presented on the facing page did in fact represent these units during most of World War II. The 107th was inactivated on 9Nov45 while the 153rd was redesignated as *Liaison Squadron* on 31May43 and similarly inactivated on the 15th of December 1945.

As noted on the facing page, squadrons comprising the 67th Observation Group did not *officially* adopt designating unit colors, the 12th and 107th Squadrons did utilize, albeit briefly, the colors indicated above. Insignia Red and Identification Yellow began appearing on the spinners of the respective squadrons Spitfire's in early summer of 1943. For some reason the 109th and 153rd Squadrons did not follow the example of there companion units, but the matter became academic as the use of these colors by the 67th and 107th was discontinued altogether by late fall of the same year.

* The 67th newly redesignated (Nov'43) 67th Tactical Reconnaissance Group was transferred from the Eighth to the Ninth Army Air Force in October 1943. Shortly after the Normandy Invasion (Jul'44) the Group was relocated to a series of air bases located on the European Continent, and would continue operations from numerous Allied A/F's in France, Belgium and Germany until wars end. The following additional squadrons would be assigned or attached to the 67thTRG shortly after transferring to the 9thAAF; **15thTRS; 30thPRS; 33rdPRS**. The 67th Tactical Reconnaissance Groups posting to Middle Wallop A/F was effected after the units transfer to the 9thAAF.

The 67th Observation/Reconnaissance Group were originally assigned approximately 48 L-4's similar to that depicted above. These were divided up evenly among the Groups four squadrons. Most of these aircraft were replaced by mid-1943 and subsequently transferred to other units, usually for liaison duty. Original fuselage code letters often remained unchanged once the aircraft had been reassigned. This can be the source of some confusion when researching photographic material for the various units to which many of these aircraft were transferred.

'SPITFIRE' MK.V
C.OCT'42-OCT'43

When the 31st and 52nd Fighter Groups were reassigned to the 12thAAF in North Africa a number of the Mk.V's assigned to these units were transferred to the 67th Observation Group. These aircraft all displayed a standard RAF tricolor paint scheme consisting of an Ocean Grey/Dark Green upper surface with a Medium Sea Grey undercarriage. Initially the 67thOG conducted operations while their 'Spits' still displayed the fuselage codes of their previous unit assignments, i.e. MX/HL/WZ of the 31stFG, or QP/WD/VF belonging to the 52ndFG. Also retained was the RAF Sky spinners and the 18in. wide Allied Fighter fuselage recognition band near the aircrafts tail. Having previously served with USAAF units a 36in. diameter Spec.No.24102-K(Amend. 3) national insignia with yellow surround were existing elements on all Mk.V's so assigned.

Also retained were the 4in. wide yellow stripes adorning the outer leading edges of both wings.

Upon receiving their squadron codes, these were applied as 24in. tall RAF Sky letters forward the national insignia on the port side fuselage, aft on the starboard. The revised AN-I-9a insignia replaced the previous version on June 29, 1943. With the introduction of this new design the squadron codes were than both positioned forward the insignia on both port and starboard sides of the fuselage.

DOUGLAS DB-7/A-20 'HAVOC'
C.FEB'43-OCT'43

This aircraft was used extensively by the Allies throughout the war and was also known as the Boston by the British. The RAF designation for these aircraft were the Havoc Mk.I, Boston Mk.II and Boston Mk.III (Intruder) series depending on armament and configuration. Upon deployment to Great Britain the 67th Observation Group received an allocation of older Mk.I Havocs from the RAF for aircraft familiarization and training purposes. These Mk.I's were delivered bearing an RAF two-color camouflage top surface configuration of Dark Earth and Dark Green. The under surfaces were handled somewhat differently depending upon an individual aircrafts previous service with the British. These consisted of an application of either an RAF Sky, black, or in some cases RAF Extra Dark Sea Grey to the lower fuselage surface areas.

8TH/USAAF
SPECIAL OPERATIONS UNITS

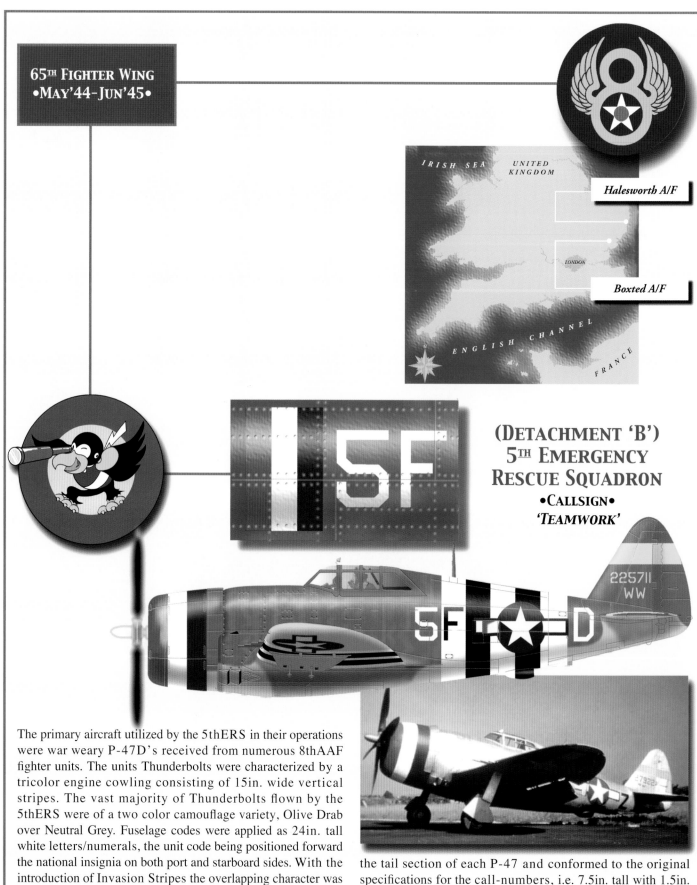

65TH FIGHTER WING
•MAY'44–JUN'45•

Halesworth A/F

Boxted A/F

IRISH SEA   UNITED KINGDOM

LONDON

ENGLISH CHANNEL

FRANCE

(DETACHMENT 'B')
5TH EMERGENCY RESCUE SQUADRON
•CALLSIGN•
'TEAMWORK'

225711
WW

5F ★ D

The primary aircraft utilized by the 5thERS in their operations were war weary P-47D's received from numerous 8thAAF fighter units. The units Thunderbolts were characterized by a tricolor engine cowling consisting of 15in. wide vertical stripes. The vast majority of Thunderbolts flown by the 5thERS were of a two color camouflage variety, Olive Drab over Neutral Grey. Fuselage codes were applied as 24in. tall white letters/numerals, the unit code being positioned forward the national insignia on both port and starboard sides. With the introduction of Invasion Stripes the overlapping character was either masked out prior to the stripes application or reapplied over the white area using black paint. The original white tail QIM's were replaced with 18in. wide yellow stripes with an additional 13.5in. of the same color applied to each wing tip. The letters 'WW' (indicating war weary status) were added to the tail section of each P-47 and conformed to the original specifications for the call-numbers, i.e. 7.5in. tall with 1.5in. character spacing. In some instances the yellow tail bands were applied in a wider width than the specified 18in. The very rare natural metal finish Thunderbolts that operated with the unit were painted using identical marking specifications with the exception that all fuselage codes/numbers were painted black.

In some instances the 5thERS insignia was applied to the engine cowling directly over the tricolor vertical group marking. With these applications a slightly lighter color shade than that found on the original artwork was used for the outer disc to facilitate better visual separation from the colored background. It is unknown just how many P-47's assigned to the 5thERS incorporated this image as 'nose art'. What is certain however is that the units insignia was in fact utilized in this manner to some extent on their P-47 engine cowlings.

For much of the war the 8thAAF had relied upon existing RAF air-sea rescue capabilities for pilot recovery missions, but by May of 1944 these RAF resources were stretched to the limit. To meet an ever increasing need, the 65th Fighter Wing formed Detachment 'B' as an 8thAAF air-sea rescue unit. On January 26, 1945, after months of invaluable service, the detachment was officially redesignated the 5th Emergency Rescue Squadron and would remain so until wars end. The formal surrender of Japan on 14Aug45 cancelled a pending transfer of the unit to the Pacific Theater following the Allied victory in Europe.

For a brief period, March through May of 1945, the 5thERS utilized numerous 'war weary' B-17G's inherited from both the 457th and 305th Bomb Groups. Those aircraft coming from the former were placed into service by the 5thERS with virtually no modifications to the existing 457thBG fuselage unit markings and bore a standard Olive Drab over Neutral Grey camouflage paint scheme. Those from the 305thBG had been employed exclusively for special night leaflet operations and displayed an ANA-622 Jet (black) under-surface in place of the standard Neutral Grey paint. As with the other B-17's these aircraft continued to display the original fuselage codes of the parent unit, however in some instances the characteristic 422ndBS 'Night Op's' black triangle tail marker was totally removed.

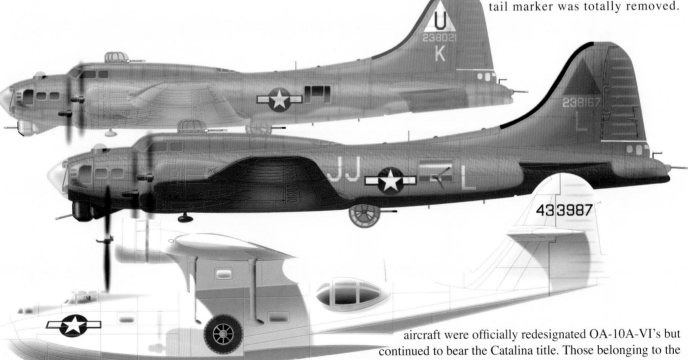

USAAF ordered numerous Navy PBY's for search and rescue operations in both the Pacific and Atlantic Theaters. The nine Catalina's that subsequently ended up assigned to the 5thERS were originally PBV-IA's built under licence by Vickers of Canada. Once turned over to the USAAF and the 5thERS these aircraft were officially redesignated OA-10A-VI's but continued to bear the Catalina title. Those belonging to the 5thERS received an overall coat of white paint, matt white on the upper hull and gloss white on the lower. From the time this unit first received these aircraft in January 1945 until wars end, the only official markings displayed were the standard AN-I-9b USAAF National Insignia on the prescribed hull and wing areas plus a black serial number on the upper tail section.

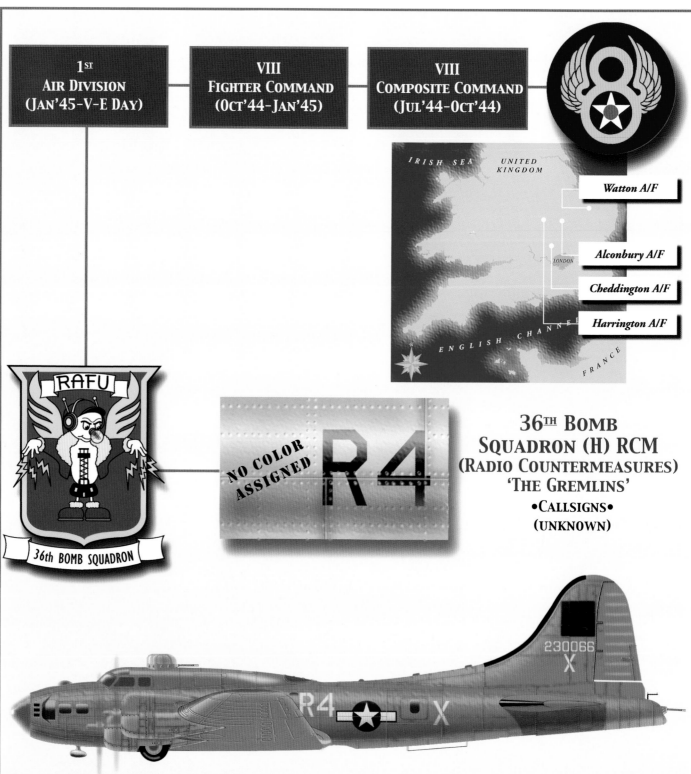

1ST AIR DIVISION (JAN'45-V-E DAY)

VIII FIGHTER COMMAND (OCT'44-JAN'45)

VIII COMPOSITE COMMAND (JUL'44-OCT'44)

Watton A/F

Alconbury A/F

Cheddington A/F

Harrington A/F

RAFU

36th BOMB SQUADRON

NO COLOR ASSIGNED

R4

36TH BOMB SQUADRON (H) RCM (RADIO COUNTERMEASURES) 'THE GREMLINS'
•CALLSIGNS•
(UNKNOWN)

The only similarity between the 36thBS(H) and other Heavy Bombardment units within the 8thAAF was in the type of aircraft utilized for their operations. The Boeing B-17 made up a majority of the squadrons inventory initially and these were 'war weary' aircraft handed over to the 36thBS from various combat units. The missions conducted by this unit involved innovative airborne electronic radar jamming equipment. These missions were dubbed with numerous esoteric code names i.e. *Freya; Small Wurzburg; Large Wurzburg; Big Ben Jostle* to name a few. In general these operations were conducted in conjunction with Allied bombing operations and were designed to disrupt the Germans radar and advanced warning systems.

These well-worn B-17's all carried a two-color, Olive Drab over Neutral Grey camouflage paint application. Tail markers indicating each aircrafts previous assignment were obliterated with a coat of either black or O.D. paint. Along with the redesignation of the squadron in August 1944 came the units R4 identification code, which were immediately applied to their Fortresses. The 36in. tall code letters were applied forward the national insignia on both sides of the fuselage in a light grey paint while individual call-letters of the same height were located aft. An additional 24in. tall call-letter was affixed to the tail section below, and usually centered on, the serial number and like the numbers applied using Identification Yellow.

36ᵀᴴ BOMB SQUADRON (H) RCM (RADAR COUNTER MEASURES)

'RAFU' : 'RADAR ALL (FOULED) UP'

ASSIGNED 8TH AAF / 2NOV43
- •STATION NO.102-ALCONBURY A/F•
  HUNTINGTONSHIRE / 6NOV43 & 28FEB45
- •STATION NO.376-WATTON A/F•
  NORFOLK / 7FEB44 (HQ ONLY)
- •STATION NO.179-HARRINGTON A/F•
  NORTHAMPTONSHIRE / 28MAR44
- •STATION NO.113-CHEDDINGTON A/F•
  BUCKINGHAMSHIRE / 14AUG44

CAMPAIGNS
- • AIR OFFENSIVE-JAPAN • ALEUTAIN ISLANDS •
- • AIR COMBAT, ASIATIC-PACIFIC THEATER •
- •AIR OFFENSIVE, EUROPE •
- • NORMANDY • NORTHERN FRANCE •
- • RHINELAND • CENTRAL EUROPE •

The early history of this unit is somewhat cloudy as 8thAAF records of the period state that the 36thBS was formed from the 803rd Bombardment Squadron (Provisional), which was originally formed at RAF Sculthrope A/F in January of 1944, and temporally attached to the 100th Bomb Group. So far so good, but these same records fail to mention that USAAF 36th Bombardment Squadron (H) was constituted on 22Dec39 and saw service with the 4thUSAAF prior to being reassigned to the 8thAAF on 21Nov43. Contemporary USAF records tie the lineage of the 36thBS(H) and 36thBS(H)RCM together and this is reflected by the Campaign Credits listed. The 803rd(P) moved to RAF Oulton A/F on 16May44 and was consolidated with Detachment 'A'/ 858thBS and the 856thBS in August '44 to form the 36th Bombardment Squadron (Heavy) Radar Countermeasures. The full European Theater of Operations deployment record of the 36thBS(H)RCM is as follows:

- •1st Bomb Division, 21Nov43
  (attached / 482nd Bomb Group, 4Dec43)
- •VIII Composite Command, 27Feb44
  (attached / 328th Service Group, 27Feb44)
  (attached / 801st Bomb Group (P), 27Mar44)
- •VIII Fighter Command, 1Oct44
- •1st Air Division, 1Jan45
  (attached / 482nd Bomb Group, 7Feb45)

Although the 36thBS(H) and 406thBS(H) were both officially transferred from Alconbury A/F to Watton A/F in February of 1945, in reality the 36thBS(H) continued to conduct ongoing operations from Alconbury A/F until it flew its final 8thAAF 'bomber assist' radar jamming mission on the 30Apr45.

One month following the formal consolidation of the unit, the newly reformed 36th Bomb Squadron (H) ceased all operations involving their B-17 Flying Fortresses and converted entirely to the use of the B-24 Liberator. From this point the 36thBS(H) operated in conjunction with the RAF on radar jamming flights through 25Nov44 when joint operations were curtailed. These joint missions were ultimately concluded altogether on 3Jan45 in order to concentrate on VHF radar screening/jamming missions for 8thAAF Bomber Command.

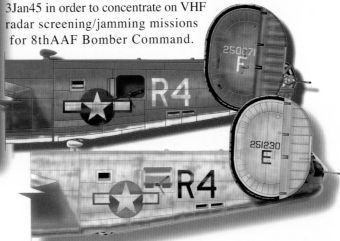

Original B-24's assigned were, like their B-17 predecessors, was weary hand-me-downs from assorted 8thAAF bomb groups. These were of a two-color camouflage type and same 36in. tall, light grey squadron codes were applied aft the gunner's window. The 24in. call-letter was positioned on each tail surface with no corresponding duplicate letter affixed to the fuselage as with the B-17's. With the introduction of natural metal finished aircraft, all letters were applied with black paint.

In addition to the heavy bombers serving with the squadron the 36thBS(H) also utilized the services of both the P-38J lightning and at least one P-51B Mustang. The former were deployed on photoreconnaissance missions while the latter provided fighter support and all were of a natural metal finish variety. Both fighter types were required to adhere to the D-Day Invasion Stripes directive and complied accordingly. The squadron codes on the P-51 were applied forward the national insignia on both sides of the fuselage, call letters aft, and all approximately 24in. in height.

With the exception of the period entailing D-Day Stripes , as depicted above, the P-38's displayed an 18in. black squadron code on both radiator housings with a call-letter of similar height affixed to both outward facing tail fin surfaces. As with the squadrons' heavy bombers, the sole distinguishing marking device carried by any of the 36thBS(H) fighters was the R4 fuselage code.

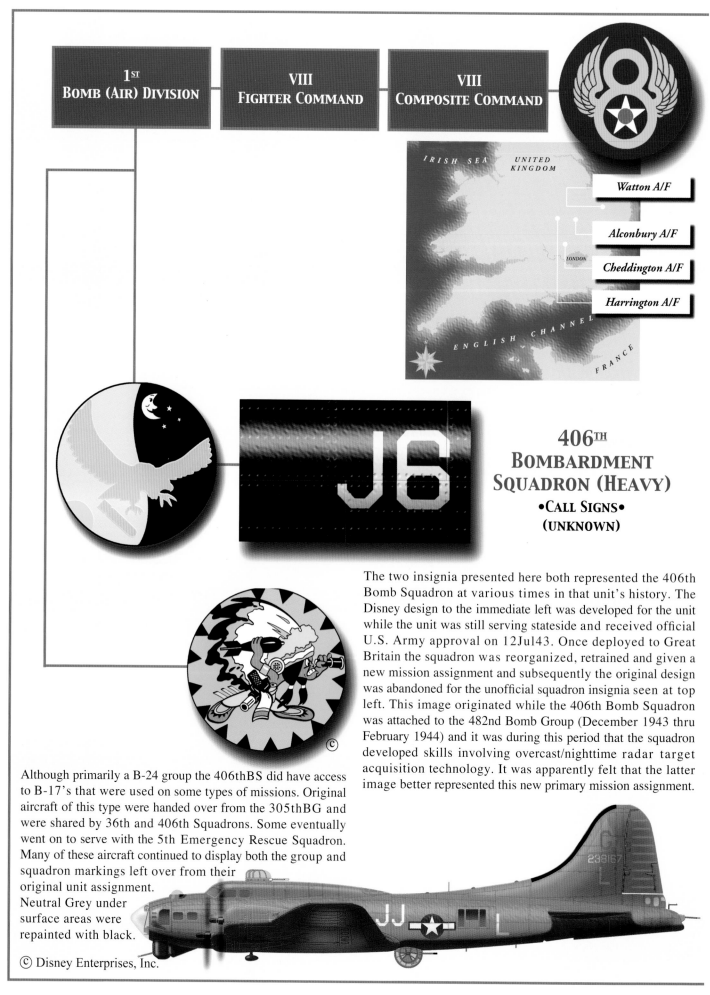

1ST BOMB (AIR) DIVISION	VIII FIGHTER COMMAND	VIII COMPOSITE COMMAND

IRISH SEA · **UNITED KINGDOM**

Watton A/F

Alconbury A/F

LONDON

Cheddington A/F

Harrington A/F

ENGLISH CHANNEL · *FRANCE*

406TH BOMBARDMENT SQUADRON (HEAVY)
•CALL SIGNS•
(UNKNOWN)

The two insignia presented here both represented the 406th Bomb Squadron at various times in that unit's history. The Disney design to the immediate left was developed for the unit while the unit was still serving stateside and received official U.S. Army approval on 12Jul43. Once deployed to Great Britain the squadron was reorganized, retrained and given a new mission assignment and subsequently the original design was abandoned for the unofficial squadron insignia seen at top left. This image originated while the 406th Bomb Squadron was attached to the 482nd Bomb Group (December 1943 thru February 1944) and it was during this period that the squadron developed skills involving overcast/nighttime radar target acquisition technology. It was apparently felt that the latter image better represented this new primary mission assignment.

Although primarily a B-24 group the 406thBS did have access to B-17's that were used on some types of missions. Original aircraft of this type were handed over from the 305thBG and were shared by 36th and 406th Squadrons. Some eventually went on to serve with the 5th Emergency Rescue Squadron. Many of these aircraft continued to display both the group and squadron markings left over from their original unit assignment. Neutral Grey under surface areas were repainted with black.

© Disney Enterprises, Inc.

122

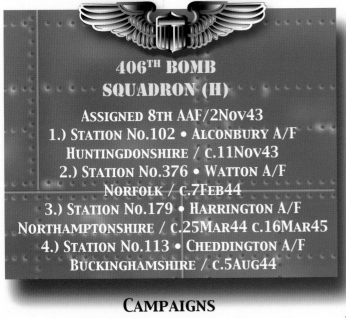

406TH BOMB SQUADRON (H)

ASSIGNED 8TH AAF/2NOV43
1.) STATION NO.102 • ALCONBURY A/F
HUNTINGDONSHIRE / C.11NOV43
2.) STATION NO.376 • WATTON A/F
NORFOLK / C.7FEB44
3.) STATION NO.179 • HARRINGTON A/F
NORTHAMPTONSHIRE / C.25MAR44 C.16MAR45
4.) STATION NO.113 • CHEDDINGTON A/F
BUCKINGHAMSHIRE / C.5AUG44

CAMPAIGNS
• ANTISUBMARINE, AMERICAN THEATER •
• ALEUTIAN ISLANDS •
• AIR COMBAT, ASIATIC-PACIFIC THEATER •
• AIR OFFENSIVE-EUROPE •
• NORMANDY • NORTHERN FRANCE •
• RHINELAND • CENTRAL EUROPE •

In September of 1943 the 422nd Bomb Squadron / 305th Bomb Group ceased normal daylight bombing operations and was ordered to concentrate on developing nighttime operational and navigational skills. The squadron would ultimately conduct nocturnal operations, mainly leaflet drops over enemy territory, until June of the following year when most of the units aircraft and crew returned to daylight operations with the 305thBG. A number of the squadron's personnel and aircraft however were reassigned and formed the nucleus of the newly organized 422nd Night Leaflet Squadron, which ultimately evolved into the 406th Bomb Squadron.

These are typical samples of printed Allied propaganda leaflets. Countless thousands of this type of material were air dropped over enemy held territory. The intent of this effort was to undermine enemy moral while simultaneously bolstering that of those living in occupied territory.

Those B-17's that continued to serve with the squadron received an overall application of black paint. The 'Double-J' fuselage code reflecting these aircrafts previous assignment with the 422nd Bomb Squadron were masked out prior to the painting process and remained affixed to each aircraft. The original triangular tail device of the 1st Bombardment (Air) Division was often initially repainted as a solid white image. This symbol was eventually eliminated from the B-17 tail sections altogether. These aircraft served both the 406th and 36th Bomb Squadrons.

B-24's carried out the vast majority of operations conducted by the 422nd Night Leaflet Squadron. The Liberators originally transferred to the 422nd were of both a painted and unpainted variety. Those arriving with a two-color camouflage paint scheme had the Neutral Grey under surfaces repainted with black. Natural metal finished B-24's received an overall application of black. This added color was probably an ANA 604 Black, Black 44 or an RAF equivalent. All were eventually standardized with ANA 622 Jet (Gloss Black), which had been specifically developed by the AAF for night aerial operations.

The insignia on these aircraft were very often 'grayed out' and carried no distinguishing unit markings for most of their service with this unit. An Identification Yellow call-letter (48in. height approx.) was applied to the tail surfaces of each ship below the aircrafts serial number. In some instances the aircraft serial number was relocated to the inward facing surfaces of the fins. The squadron 'J6' code appeared very late in the war. It was eventually painted as 48in. tall Identification Yellow letters aft the waist gunner's station on both sides of the aircrafts fuselage.

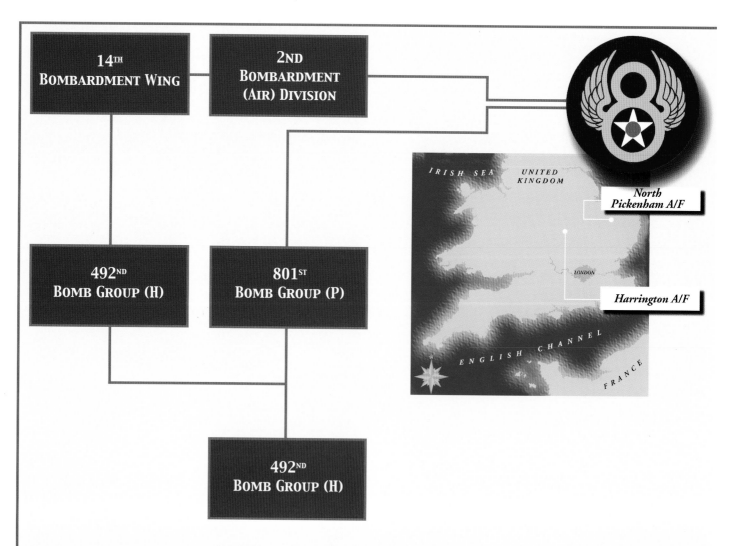

14TH BOMBARDMENT WING

2ND BOMBARDMENT (AIR) DIVISION

492ND BOMB GROUP (H)

801ST BOMB GROUP (P)

492ND BOMB GROUP (H)

North Pickenham A/F

Harrington A/F

IRISH SEA — UNITED KINGDOM — LONDON — ENGLISH CHANNEL — FRANCE

The story of the 801st/492nd Bomb Group(s) is really that of three distinctly seperate units, which ultimately merged into one. The original 492BG(H) was activated in the United States on 1Oct43 and was deployed to Great Britain and subsequently stationed at North Pickenham A/F on 18Apr44. As one of the last heavy bombardment groups to arrive in England the 492nd was considered to be one of the best trained and best equipped bomb units within the 8thAAF structure, which makes this units battle history all the more perplexing. After only 89 days of actual operations the 492nd Bomb Group (H) was removed from combat status having sustained a combat causality rate of approximately 117%. To put this figure into some sort of perspective, the average casualty rate within the 8thAAF at this time was approximately 16 per 1000 combat personal, the ratio within the 492ndBG was 442 casualties per 1000 combat personnel. The 492nd was not to recover from these devastating losses and in fact this unit has the dubious distinction of being the only formally established group in the annals of United States air operations to have been disbanded as a direct result of combat losses. And so it was that in August 1944 the 492nd BG(H) was dismantled, its full inventory of aircraft, equipment and personnel reassigned to numerous other bomb groups within the 8thAAF structure. The stage was now set for the rebirth of this unit, and while the name would remain the same, the primary mission of the new 492nd was to be entirely different.

In early May of 1944 the 801st Bomb Group (Provisional) was created by combining the resources of both the 36th and 406th Bomb Squadrons at Harrington Airfield. The missions of this newly formed unit was to expand upon the Carpetbagger operations begun earlier that same year. These missions were top secret in nature and even though the new unit was officially structured within the 8thAAF, actual operational control was maintained by the Office of Strategic Services (OSS) forerunner of today's Central Intelligence Agency. Still in its infancy at this stage of its history the OSS was sparsely funded and lacking many resources and thus largely dependent upon the military establishment for the much of the infrastructure necessary to conduct its operations. While the Carpetbagger missions were proving highly successful in the Allied effort against German occupied Western Europe, a problem arose concerning the OSS's partner in the Carpetbagger effort, namely the 8thAAF itself. By forming the 801stBG(P) and several other 'Provisional' units, the Eighth had exceeded its Congressionally authorized component strength. Not inclined to discontinue or disrupt the highly effective Carpetbagger operations, HQ/8thAAF took advantage of the recent breakup of the unfortunate 492ndBG and transferred the name along with a handful of select personnel to Harrington A/F. Although the 492nd would continue to bear the BG (H) designation, its role in the war was to become much more complex.

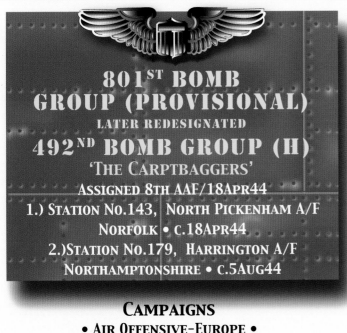

801ST BOMB GROUP (PROVISIONAL)

LATER REDESIGNATED

492ND BOMB GROUP (H)

'THE CARPTBAGGERS'

ASSIGNED 8TH AAF/18APR44

1.) STATION NO.143, NORTH PICKENHAM A/F
NORFOLK • C.18APR44
2.) STATION NO.179, HARRINGTON A/F
NORTHAMPTONSHIRE • C.5AUG44

CAMPAIGNS

- AIR OFFENSIVE-EUROPE •
- NORMANDY • NORTHERN FRANCE •
- SOUTHREN FRANCE • RHINELAND •
- CENTRAL EUROPE •

Although the exploits of the 492nd Bombardment Group (Heavy) and their Carpetbagger missions make for fascinating reading the very nature of these operations necessitated a low profile image and thus, from a strictly visual perspective, the 492nd makes for anything but an exciting subject. As near as can be determined to date, no official or unofficial insignia for the 'second' 492ndBG nor any of its components ever existed.

The 492ndBG(H) utilized a wide assortment of aircraft for its operations and in fact were the sole unit within the 8thAAF to include the Douglas A-26 'Invader' within its inventory. The B-24 inventory of the original 492nd had been all of a natural metal finished variety but those aircraft that ultimately remained with the reformed Group, as well as those that followed, were immediately painted. The upper surfaces of the 'Libs received a coat of standard Dark Olive Drab while the under-surface was painted with a flat black. A few of this type of aircraft were later reportedly painted an overall ANA 622 Jet (black) but photographic evidence of this is as yet forthcoming. The aircraft serial numbers were relocated to the upper inside facing surface areas and applied with either Identification Yellow or Insignia Red. A 24in. tall yellow call-letter was the only distinguishing mark applied to these particular aircraft. The Douglas C-47 'Skytrains' utilized by the 492ndBG received a similar exterior paint treatment however in this instance the original tail number remained and was surmounted with a 24in. tall call-letter. The Douglas A-26 'Invaders' were painted in overall ANA 622 Jet (black) with the tail number and accompanying 18in. tall call-letter applied with Insignia Red. The British de Havilland 'Mosquito' PR XVI's flown by the 492ndBG on its own Red Stocking missions were borrowed from the 654th Bomb Squadron (Special) / 25th Bomb Group (Reconnaissance).

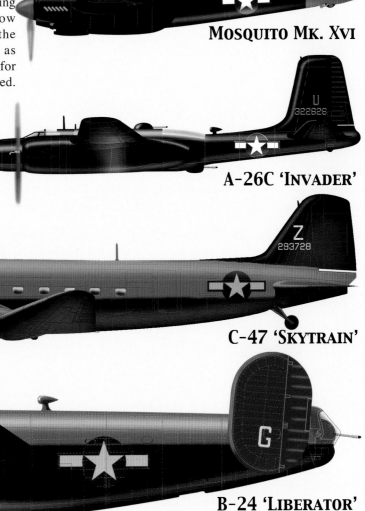

MOSQUITO MK. XVI

A-26C 'INVADER'

C-47 'SKYTRAIN'

B-24 'LIBERATOR'

USAAF/ Eighth Air Force
•Fighter groups & Squadron Assignments•

1st Fighter Group	27th Fighter Squadron	71st Fighter Squadron	94th Fighter Squadron
4th Fighter Group	334th Fighter Squadron	335th Fighter Squadron	336th Fighter Squadron
14th Fighter Group	48th Fighter Squadron	49th Fighter Squadron	50th Fighter Squadron
20th Fighter Group	55th Fighter Squadron	77th Fighter Squadron	79th Fighter Squadron
31st Fighter Group	307th Fighter Squadron	308th Fighter Squadron	309th Fighter Squadron
52nd Fighter Group	2nd Fighter Squadron	4th Fighter Squadron	5th Fighter Squadron
55th Fighter Group	38th Fighter Squadron	338th Fighter Squadron	343rd Fighter Squadron
56th Fighter Group	61st Fighter Squadron	62nd Fighter Squadron	63rd Fighter Squadron
78th Fighter Group	82nd Fighter Squadron	83rd Fighter Squadron	84th Fighter Squadron
339th Fighter Group	503rd Fighter Squadron	504th Fighter Squadron	505th Fighter Squadron
352nd Fighter Group	328th Fighter Squadron	486th Fighter Squadron	487th Fighter Squadron
353rd Fighter Group	350th Fighter Squadron	351st Fighter Squadron	352nd Fighter Squadron
355th Fighter Group	354th Fighter Squadron	357th Fighter Squadron	358th Fighter Squadron
356th Fighter Group	359th Fighter Squadron	360th Fighter Squadron	361st Fighter Squadron
357th Fighter Group	362nd Fighter Squadron	363rd Fighter Squadron	364th Fighter Squadron
358th Fighter Group	365th Fighter Squadron	366th Fighter Squadron	367th Fighter Squadron
359th Fighter Group	368th Fighter Squadron	369th Fighter Squadron	370th Fighter Squadron
361st Fighter Group	374th Fighter Squadron	375th Fighter Squadron	376th Fighter Squadron
364th Fighter Group	383rd Fighter Squadron	384th Fighter Squadron	385th Fighter Squadron
479th Fighter Group	334th Fighter Squadron	435th Fighter Squadron	436th Fighter Squadron
1st Scouting Force	Detachment/383rdFS	Detachment/384thFS	Detachment/385thFS
2nd Scouting Force	Detachment/354thFS	Detachment/357thFS	Detachment/388thFS
3rd Scouting Force	Detachment/38thFS	Detachment/338thFS	Detachment/343rdFS

ORGANIZATION & DEPLOYMENT
UNITED STATES EIGHTH ARMY AIR FORCE

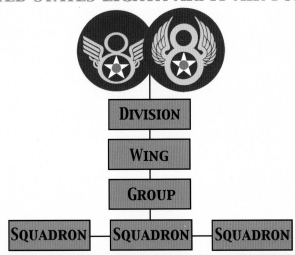

DIVISION

WING

GROUP

SQUADRON — SQUADRON — SQUADRON

U.S. Army Air Force Bases
East Anglia
England
June, 1944

PETERSBOROUGH

NORWICH

CAMBRIDGE

NORTHAMPTON

BEDFORD

IPSWICH

GLOCHESTER

CHELMSFORD

LONDON

N

0   10   20
Miles

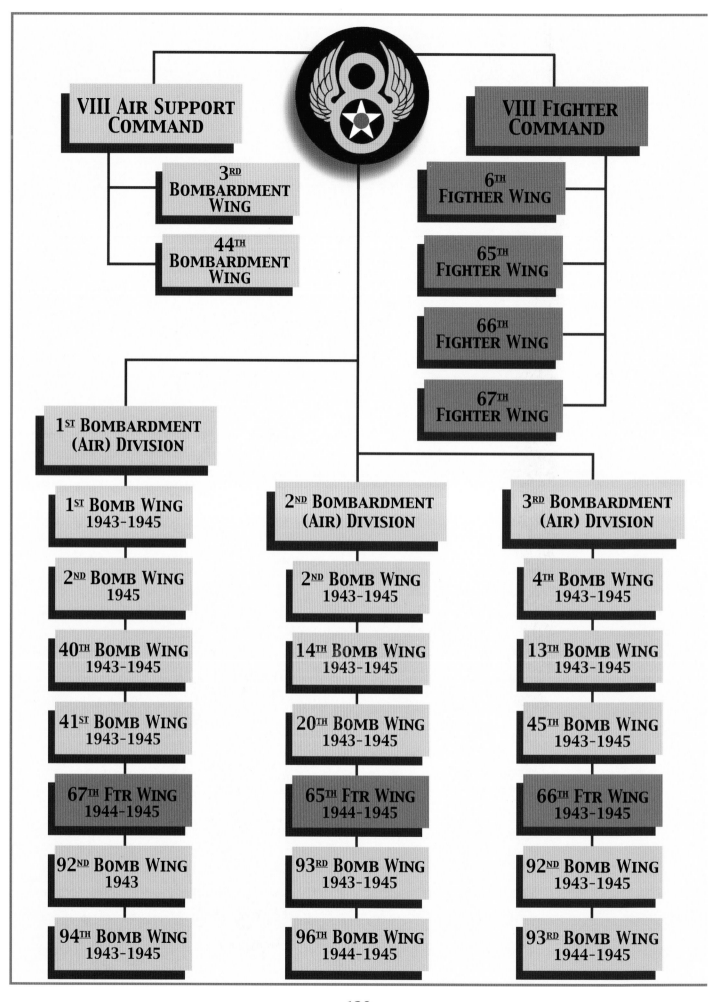

VIII AIR SUPPORT COMMAND

3RD BOMBARDMENT WING

44TH BOMBARDMENT WING

VIII FIGHTER COMMAND

6TH FIGHTER WING

65TH FIGHTER WING

66TH FIGHTER WING

67TH FIGHTER WING

1ST BOMBARDMENT (AIR) DIVISION

1ST BOMB WING
1943-1945

2ND BOMB WING
1945

40TH BOMB WING
1943-1945

41ST BOMB WING
1943-1945

67TH FTR WING
1944-1945

92ND BOMB WING
1943

94TH BOMB WING
1943-1945

2ND BOMBARDMENT (AIR) DIVISION

2ND BOMB WING
1943-1945

14TH BOMB WING
1943-1945

20TH BOMB WING
1943-1945

65TH FTR WING
1944-1945

93RD BOMB WING
1943-1945

96TH BOMB WING
1944-1945

3RD BOMBARDMENT (AIR) DIVISION

4TH BOMB WING
1943-1945

13TH BOMB WING
1943-1945

45TH BOMB WING
1943-1945

66TH FTR WING
1943-1945

92ND BOMB WING
1943-1945

93RD BOMB WING
1944-1945

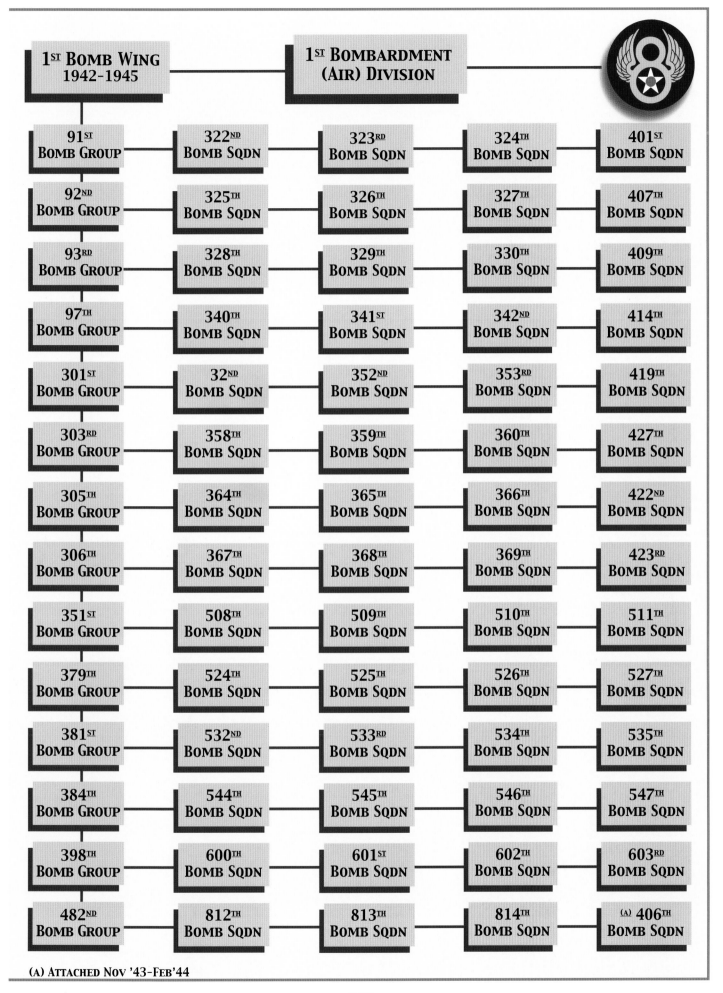

1ST BOMB WING 1942-1945	**1ST BOMBARDMENT (AIR) DIVISION**			
91ST BOMB GROUP	**322ND BOMB SQDN**	**323RD BOMB SQDN**	**324TH BOMB SQDN**	**401ST BOMB SQDN**
92ND BOMB GROUP	**325TH BOMB SQDN**	**326TH BOMB SQDN**	**327TH BOMB SQDN**	**407TH BOMB SQDN**
93RD BOMB GROUP	**328TH BOMB SQDN**	**329TH BOMB SQDN**	**330TH BOMB SQDN**	**409TH BOMB SQDN**
97TH BOMB GROUP	**340TH BOMB SQDN**	**341ST BOMB SQDN**	**342ND BOMB SQDN**	**414TH BOMB SQDN**
301ST BOMB GROUP	**32ND BOMB SQDN**	**352ND BOMB SQDN**	**353RD BOMB SQDN**	**419TH BOMB SQDN**
303RD BOMB GROUP	**358TH BOMB SQDN**	**359TH BOMB SQDN**	**360TH BOMB SQDN**	**427TH BOMB SQDN**
305TH BOMB GROUP	**364TH BOMB SQDN**	**365TH BOMB SQDN**	**366TH BOMB SQDN**	**422ND BOMB SQDN**
306TH BOMB GROUP	**367TH BOMB SQDN**	**368TH BOMB SQDN**	**369TH BOMB SQDN**	**423RD BOMB SQDN**
351ST BOMB GROUP	**508TH BOMB SQDN**	**509TH BOMB SQDN**	**510TH BOMB SQDN**	**511TH BOMB SQDN**
379TH BOMB GROUP	**524TH BOMB SQDN**	**525TH BOMB SQDN**	**526TH BOMB SQDN**	**527TH BOMB SQDN**
381ST BOMB GROUP	**532ND BOMB SQDN**	**533RD BOMB SQDN**	**534TH BOMB SQDN**	**535TH BOMB SQDN**
384TH BOMB GROUP	**544TH BOMB SQDN**	**545TH BOMB SQDN**	**546TH BOMB SQDN**	**547TH BOMB SQDN**
398TH BOMB GROUP	**600TH BOMB SQDN**	**601ST BOMB SQDN**	**602TH BOMB SQDN**	**603RD BOMB SQDN**
482ND BOMB GROUP	**812TH BOMB SQDN**	**813TH BOMB SQDN**	**814TH BOMB SQDN**	**(A) 406TH BOMB SQDN**

(A) ATTACHED NOV '43-FEB'44

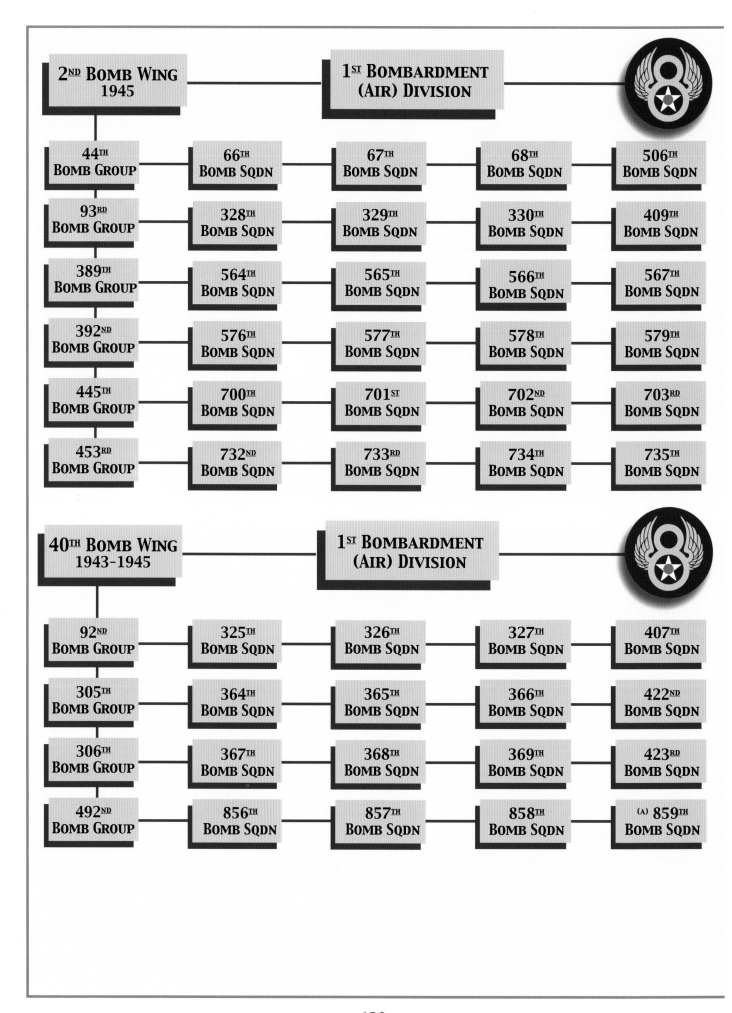

2ND BOMB WING 1945 — **1ST BOMBARDMENT (AIR) DIVISION**

44TH BOMB GROUP	66TH BOMB SQDN	67TH BOMB SQDN	68TH BOMB SQDN	506TH BOMB SQDN
93RD BOMB GROUP	328TH BOMB SQDN	329TH BOMB SQDN	330TH BOMB SQDN	409TH BOMB SQDN
389TH BOMB GROUP	564TH BOMB SQDN	565TH BOMB SQDN	566TH BOMB SQDN	567TH BOMB SQDN
392ND BOMB GROUP	576TH BOMB SQDN	577TH BOMB SQDN	578TH BOMB SQDN	579TH BOMB SQDN
445TH BOMB GROUP	700TH BOMB SQDN	701ST BOMB SQDN	702ND BOMB SQDN	703RD BOMB SQDN
453RD BOMB GROUP	732ND BOMB SQDN	733RD BOMB SQDN	734TH BOMB SQDN	735TH BOMB SQDN

40TH BOMB WING 1943-1945 — **1ST BOMBARDMENT (AIR) DIVISION**

92ND BOMB GROUP	325TH BOMB SQDN	326TH BOMB SQDN	327TH BOMB SQDN	407TH BOMB SQDN
305TH BOMB GROUP	364TH BOMB SQDN	365TH BOMB SQDN	366TH BOMB SQDN	422ND BOMB SQDN
306TH BOMB GROUP	367TH BOMB SQDN	368TH BOMB SQDN	369TH BOMB SQDN	423RD BOMB SQDN
492ND BOMB GROUP	856TH BOMB SQDN	857TH BOMB SQDN	858TH BOMB SQDN	(A) 859TH BOMB SQDN

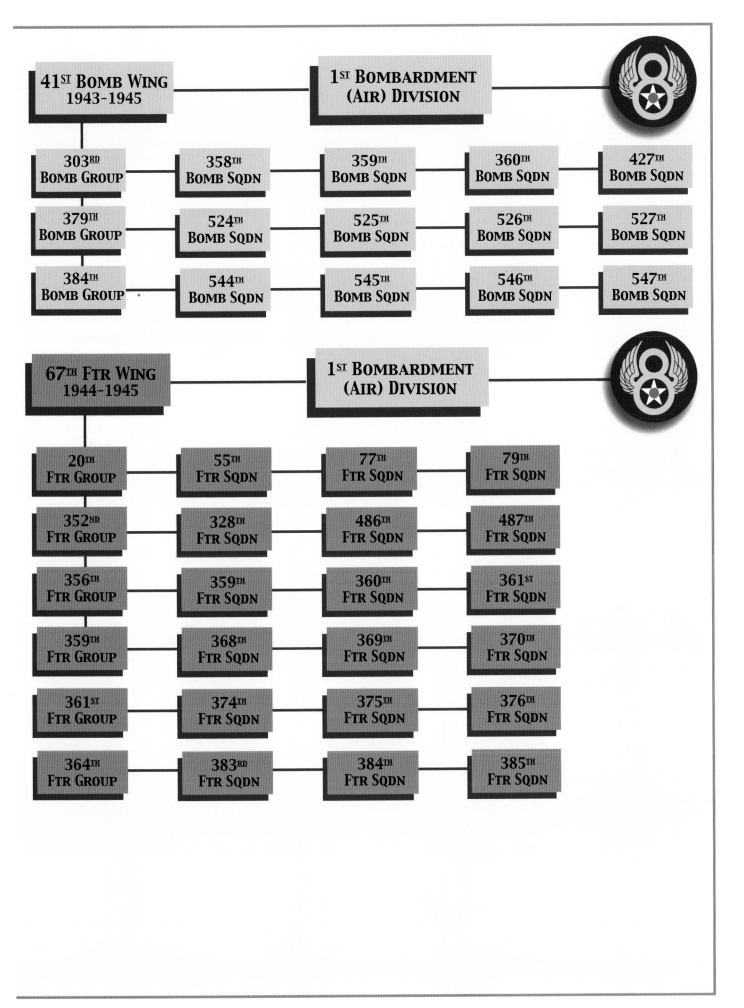

41ST BOMB WING 1943-1945 — **1ST BOMBARDMENT (AIR) DIVISION**

303RD BOMB GROUP	358TH BOMB SQDN	359TH BOMB SQDN	360TH BOMB SQDN	427TH BOMB SQDN
379TH BOMB GROUP	524TH BOMB SQDN	525TH BOMB SQDN	526TH BOMB SQDN	527TH BOMB SQDN
384TH BOMB GROUP	544TH BOMB SQDN	545TH BOMB SQDN	546TH BOMB SQDN	547TH BOMB SQDN

67TH FTR WING 1944-1945 — **1ST BOMBARDMENT (AIR) DIVISION**

20TH FTR GROUP	55TH FTR SQDN	77TH FTR SQDN	79TH FTR SQDN
352ND FTR GROUP	328TH FTR SQDN	486TH FTR SQDN	487TH FTR SQDN
356TH FTR GROUP	359TH FTR SQDN	360TH FTR SQDN	361ST FTR SQDN
359TH FTR GROUP	368TH FTR SQDN	369TH FTR SQDN	370TH FTR SQDN
361ST FTR GROUP	374TH FTR SQDN	375TH FTR SQDN	376TH FTR SQDN
364TH FTR GROUP	383RD FTR SQDN	384TH FTR SQDN	385TH FTR SQDN

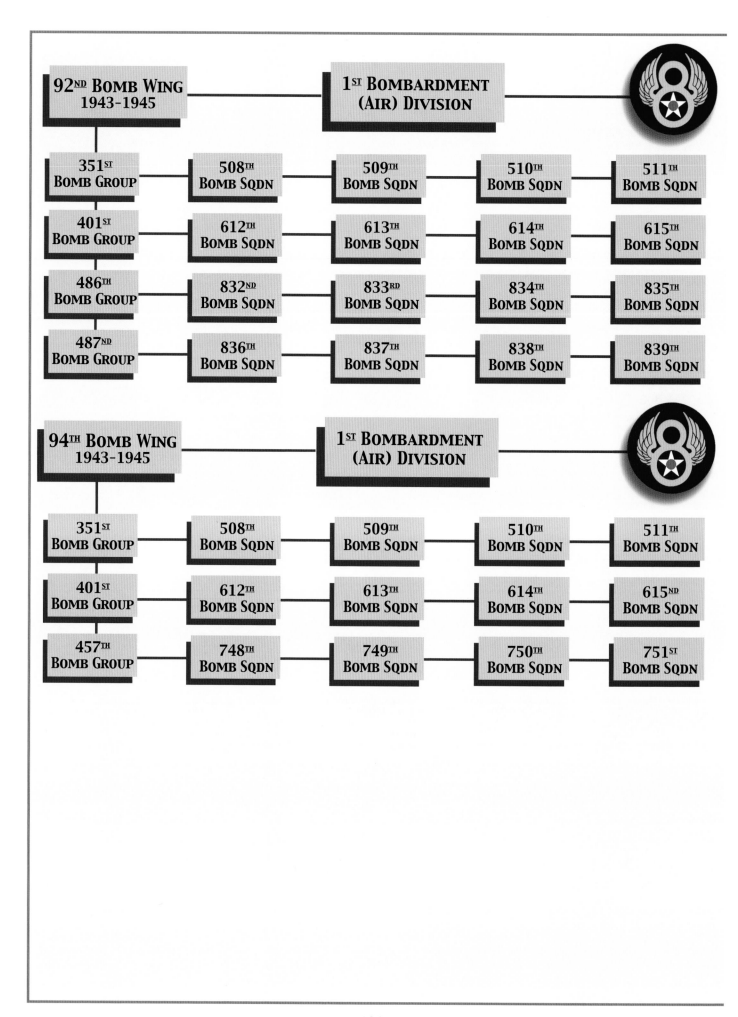

92ND BOMB WING 1943-1945 — **1ST BOMBARDMENT (AIR) DIVISION**

- **351ST BOMB GROUP** — 508TH BOMB SQDN — 509TH BOMB SQDN — 510TH BOMB SQDN — 511TH BOMB SQDN
- **401ST BOMB GROUP** — 612TH BOMB SQDN — 613TH BOMB SQDN — 614TH BOMB SQDN — 615TH BOMB SQDN
- **486TH BOMB GROUP** — 832ND BOMB SQDN — 833RD BOMB SQDN — 834TH BOMB SQDN — 835TH BOMB SQDN
- **487ND BOMB GROUP** — 836TH BOMB SQDN — 837TH BOMB SQDN — 838TH BOMB SQDN — 839TH BOMB SQDN

94TH BOMB WING 1943-1945 — **1ST BOMBARDMENT (AIR) DIVISION**

- **351ST BOMB GROUP** — 508TH BOMB SQDN — 509TH BOMB SQDN — 510TH BOMB SQDN — 511TH BOMB SQDN
- **401ST BOMB GROUP** — 612TH BOMB SQDN — 613TH BOMB SQDN — 614TH BOMB SQDN — 615ND BOMB SQDN
- **457TH BOMB GROUP** — 748TH BOMB SQDN — 749TH BOMB SQDN — 750TH BOMB SQDN — 751ST BOMB SQDN

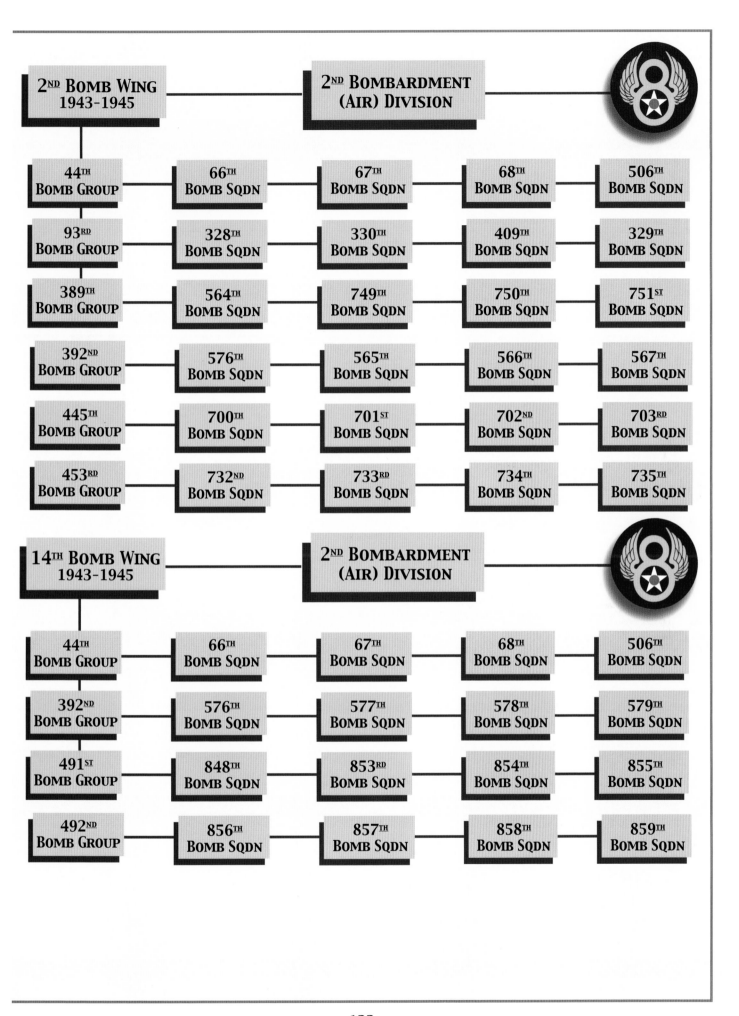

2ND BOMB WING 1943-1945 — **2ND BOMBARDMENT (AIR) DIVISION**

44TH BOMB GROUP	66TH BOMB SQDN	67TH BOMB SQDN	68TH BOMB SQDN	506TH BOMB SQDN
93RD BOMB GROUP	328TH BOMB SQDN	330TH BOMB SQDN	409TH BOMB SQDN	329TH BOMB SQDN
389TH BOMB GROUP	564TH BOMB SQDN	749TH BOMB SQDN	750TH BOMB SQDN	751ST BOMB SQDN
392ND BOMB GROUP	576TH BOMB SQDN	565TH BOMB SQDN	566TH BOMB SQDN	567TH BOMB SQDN
445TH BOMB GROUP	700TH BOMB SQDN	701ST BOMB SQDN	702ND BOMB SQDN	703RD BOMB SQDN
453RD BOMB GROUP	732ND BOMB SQDN	733RD BOMB SQDN	734TH BOMB SQDN	735TH BOMB SQDN

14TH BOMB WING 1943-1945 — **2ND BOMBARDMENT (AIR) DIVISION**

44TH BOMB GROUP	66TH BOMB SQDN	67TH BOMB SQDN	68TH BOMB SQDN	506TH BOMB SQDN
392ND BOMB GROUP	576TH BOMB SQDN	577TH BOMB SQDN	578TH BOMB SQDN	579TH BOMB SQDN
491ST BOMB GROUP	848TH BOMB SQDN	853RD BOMB SQDN	854TH BOMB SQDN	855TH BOMB SQDN
492ND BOMB GROUP	856TH BOMB SQDN	857TH BOMB SQDN	858TH BOMB SQDN	859TH BOMB SQDN

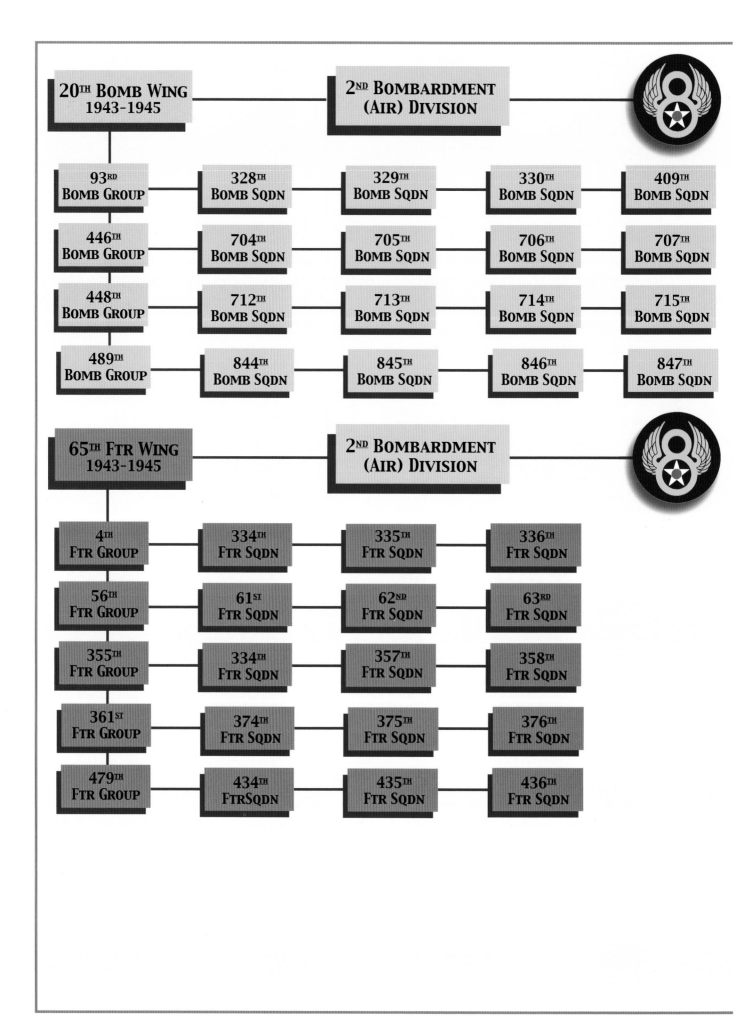

20TH BOMB WING 1943-1945 — **2ND BOMBARDMENT (AIR) DIVISION**

- **93RD BOMB GROUP** — 328TH BOMB SQDN — 329TH BOMB SQDN — 330TH BOMB SQDN — 409TH BOMB SQDN
- **446TH BOMB GROUP** — 704TH BOMB SQDN — 705TH BOMB SQDN — 706TH BOMB SQDN — 707TH BOMB SQDN
- **448TH BOMB GROUP** — 712TH BOMB SQDN — 713TH BOMB SQDN — 714TH BOMB SQDN — 715TH BOMB SQDN
- **489TH BOMB GROUP** — 844TH BOMB SQDN — 845TH BOMB SQDN — 846TH BOMB SQDN — 847TH BOMB SQDN

65TH FTR WING 1943-1945 — **2ND BOMBARDMENT (AIR) DIVISION**

- **4TH FTR GROUP** — 334TH FTR SQDN — 335TH FTR SQDN — 336TH FTR SQDN
- **56TH FTR GROUP** — 61ST FTR SQDN — 62ND FTR SQDN — 63RD FTR SQDN
- **355TH FTR GROUP** — 334TH FTR SQDN — 357TH FTR SQDN — 358TH FTR SQDN
- **361ST FTR GROUP** — 374TH FTR SQDN — 375TH FTR SQDN — 376TH FTR SQDN
- **479TH FTR GROUP** — 434TH FTRSQDN — 435TH FTR SQDN — 436TH FTR SQDN

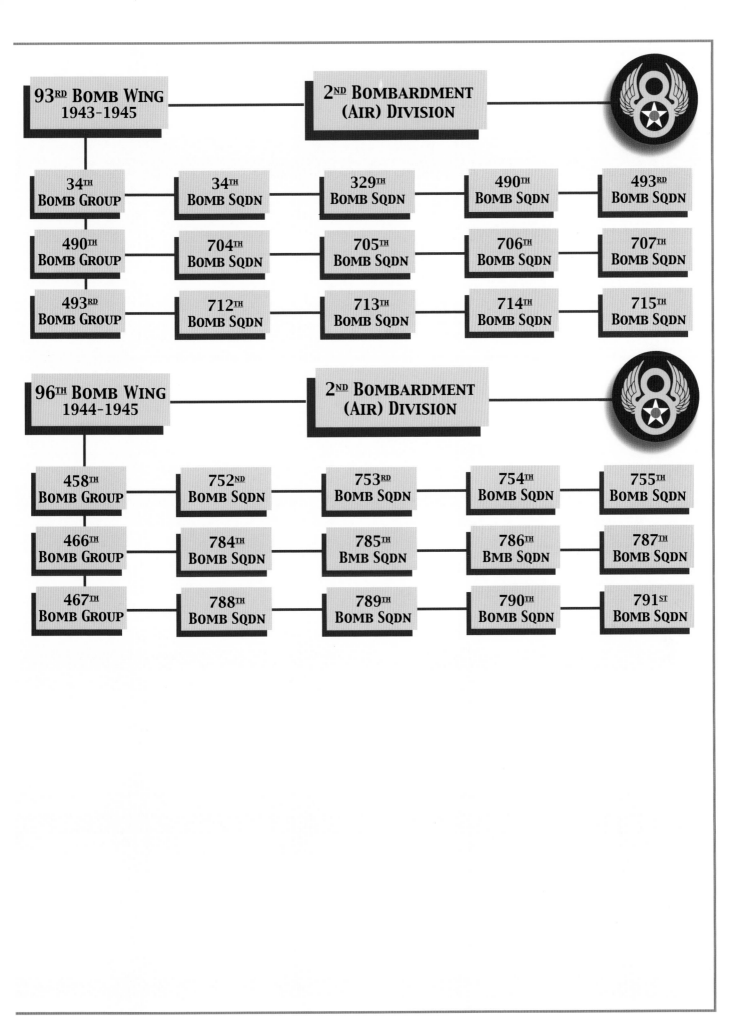

93RD BOMB WING 1943-1945 — **2ND BOMBARDMENT (AIR) DIVISION**

34TH BOMB GROUP	34TH BOMB SQDN	329TH BOMB SQDN	490TH BOMB SQDN	493RD BOMB SQDN
490TH BOMB GROUP	704TH BOMB SQDN	705TH BOMB SQDN	706TH BOMB SQDN	707TH BOMB SQDN
493RD BOMB GROUP	712TH BOMB SQDN	713TH BOMB SQDN	714TH BOMB SQDN	715TH BOMB SQDN

96TH BOMB WING 1944-1945 — **2ND BOMBARDMENT (AIR) DIVISION**

458TH BOMB GROUP	752ND BOMB SQDN	753RD BOMB SQDN	754TH BOMB SQDN	755TH BOMB SQDN
466TH BOMB GROUP	784TH BOMB SQDN	785TH BMB SQDN	786TH BMB SQDN	787TH BOMB SQDN
467TH BOMB GROUP	788TH BOMB SQDN	789TH BOMB SQDN	790TH BOMB SQDN	791ST BOMB SQDN

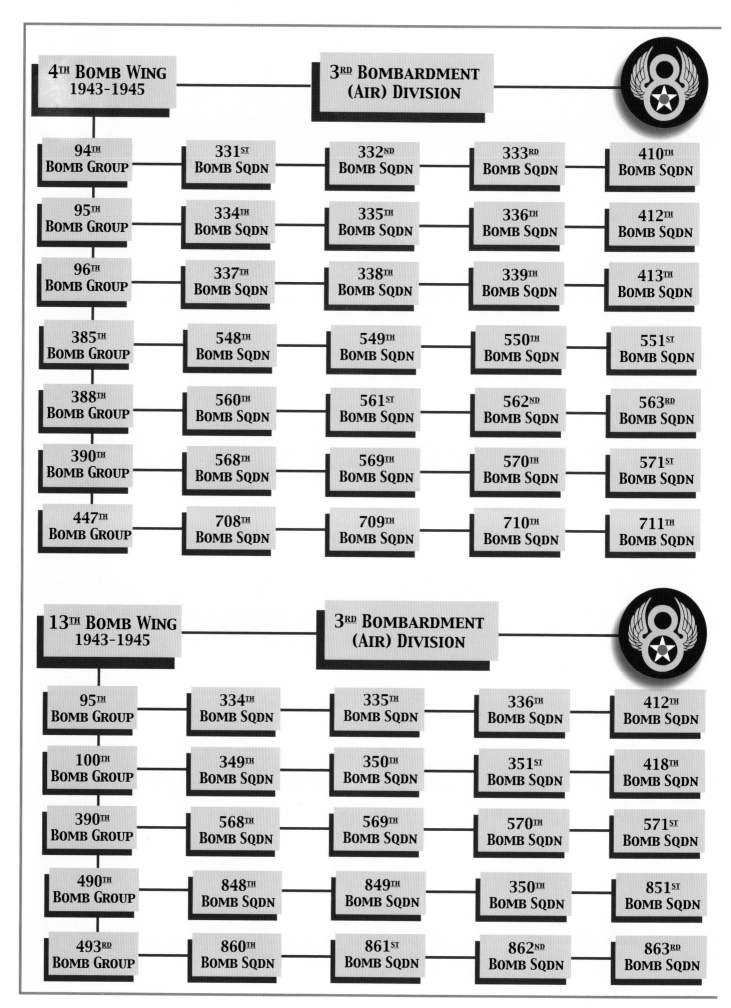

4TH BOMB WING 1943-1945 — **3RD BOMBARDMENT (AIR) DIVISION**

94TH BOMB GROUP	331ST BOMB SQDN	332ND BOMB SQDN	333RD BOMB SQDN	410TH BOMB SQDN
95TH BOMB GROUP	334TH BOMB SQDN	335TH BOMB SQDN	336TH BOMB SQDN	412TH BOMB SQDN
96TH BOMB GROUP	337TH BOMB SQDN	338TH BOMB SQDN	339TH BOMB SQDN	413TH BOMB SQDN
385TH BOMB GROUP	548TH BOMB SQDN	549TH BOMB SQDN	550TH BOMB SQDN	551ST BOMB SQDN
388TH BOMB GROUP	560TH BOMB SQDN	561ST BOMB SQDN	562ND BOMB SQDN	563RD BOMB SQDN
390TH BOMB GROUP	568TH BOMB SQDN	569TH BOMB SQDN	570TH BOMB SQDN	571ST BOMB SQDN
447TH BOMB GROUP	708TH BOMB SQDN	709TH BOMB SQDN	710TH BOMB SQDN	711TH BOMB SQDN

13TH BOMB WING 1943-1945 — **3RD BOMBARDMENT (AIR) DIVISION**

95TH BOMB GROUP	334TH BOMB SQDN	335TH BOMB SQDN	336TH BOMB SQDN	412TH BOMB SQDN
100TH BOMB GROUP	349TH BOMB SQDN	350TH BOMB SQDN	351ST BOMB SQDN	418TH BOMB SQDN
390TH BOMB GROUP	568TH BOMB SQDN	569TH BOMB SQDN	570TH BOMB SQDN	571ST BOMB SQDN
490TH BOMB GROUP	848TH BOMB SQDN	849TH BOMB SQDN	350TH BOMB SQDN	851ST BOMB SQDN
493RD BOMB GROUP	860TH BOMB SQDN	861ST BOMB SQDN	862ND BOMB SQDN	863RD BOMB SQDN

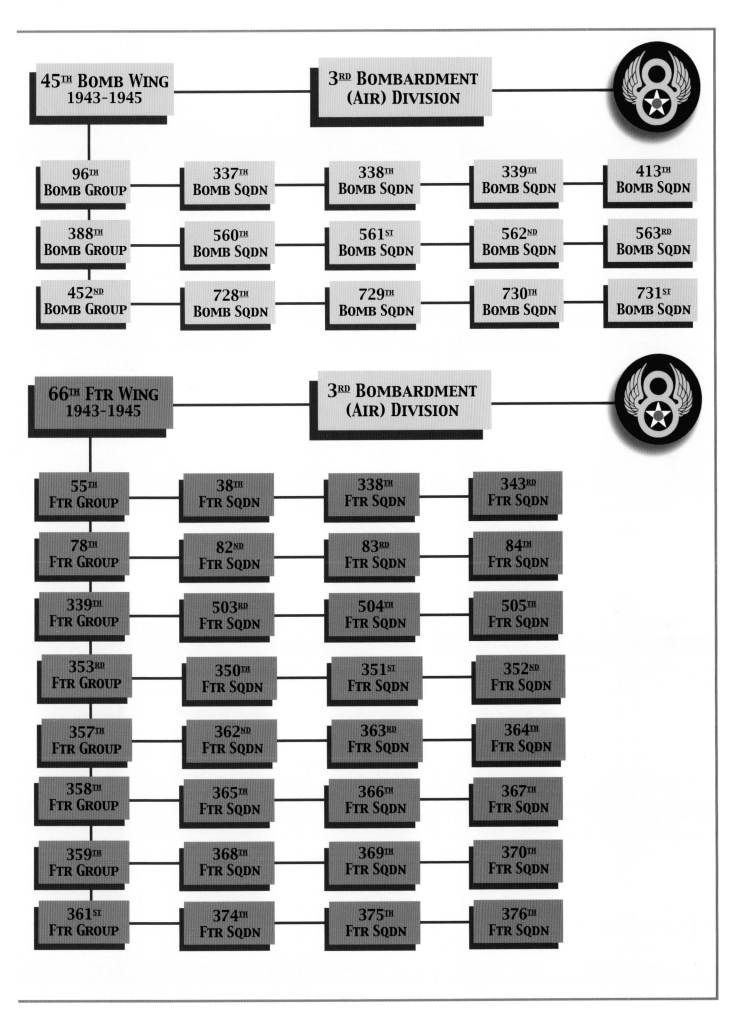

45TH BOMB WING 1943-1945 — **3RD BOMBARDMENT (AIR) DIVISION**

- **96TH BOMB GROUP** — 337TH BOMB SQDN — 338TH BOMB SQDN — 339TH BOMB SQDN — 413TH BOMB SQDN
- **388TH BOMB GROUP** — 560TH BOMB SQDN — 561ST BOMB SQDN — 562ND BOMB SQDN — 563RD BOMB SQDN
- **452ND BOMB GROUP** — 728TH BOMB SQDN — 729TH BOMB SQDN — 730TH BOMB SQDN — 731ST BOMB SQDN

66TH FTR WING 1943-1945 — **3RD BOMBARDMENT (AIR) DIVISION**

- **55TH FTR GROUP** — 38TH FTR SQDN — 338TH FTR SQDN — 343RD FTR SQDN
- **78TH FTR GROUP** — 82ND FTR SQDN — 83RD FTR SQDN — 84TH FTR SQDN
- **339TH FTR GROUP** — 503RD FTR SQDN — 504TH FTR SQDN — 505TH FTR SQDN
- **353RD FTR GROUP** — 350TH FTR SQDN — 351ST FTR SQDN — 352ND FTR SQDN
- **357TH FTR GROUP** — 362ND FTR SQDN — 363RD FTR SQDN — 364TH FTR SQDN
- **358TH FTR GROUP** — 365TH FTR SQDN — 366TH FTR SQDN — 367TH FTR SQDN
- **359TH FTR GROUP** — 368TH FTR SQDN — 369TH FTR SQDN — 370TH FTR SQDN
- **361ST FTR GROUP** — 374TH FTR SQDN — 375TH FTR SQDN — 376TH FTR SQDN

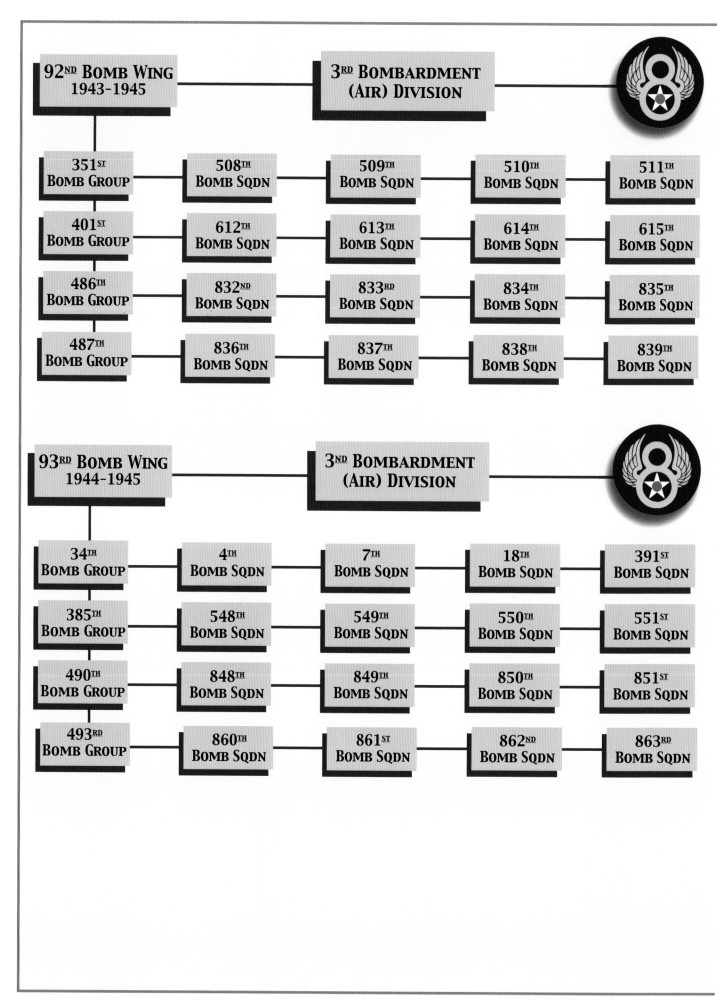

92ND BOMB WING
1943-1945

3RD BOMBARDMENT (AIR) DIVISION

351ST BOMB GROUP	508TH BOMB SQDN	509TH BOMB SQDN	510TH BOMB SQDN	511TH BOMB SQDN
401ST BOMB GROUP	612TH BOMB SQDN	613TH BOMB SQDN	614TH BOMB SQDN	615TH BOMB SQDN
486TH BOMB GROUP	832ND BOMB SQDN	833RD BOMB SQDN	834TH BOMB SQDN	835TH BOMB SQDN
487TH BOMB GROUP	836TH BOMB SQDN	837TH BOMB SQDN	838TH BOMB SQDN	839TH BOMB SQDN

93RD BOMB WING
1944-1945

3ND BOMBARDMENT (AIR) DIVISION

34TH BOMB GROUP	4TH BOMB SQDN	7TH BOMB SQDN	18TH BOMB SQDN	391ST BOMB SQDN
385TH BOMB GROUP	548TH BOMB SQDN	549TH BOMB SQDN	550TH BOMB SQDN	551ST BOMB SQDN
490TH BOMB GROUP	848TH BOMB SQDN	849TH BOMB SQDN	850TH BOMB SQDN	851ST BOMB SQDN
493RD BOMB GROUP	860TH BOMB SQDN	861ST BOMB SQDN	862ND BOMB SQDN	863RD BOMB SQDN

ABBREVIATIONS

AAA	Anti-Aircraft Artillery
AAF	Army Air Force
AB	Air Base
AAB	Army Air Base
A/C	Aircraft
AD	Air Division
Air.Div	Air Division
A/D	Air Depot
AEF	American Expeditionary Force
AF	Air Force
A/F	Airfield
ANA	Army-Navy Aeronautical
AS / Antisub	Anti-Submarine
A/S	Airstrip
ATO	American Theater of Operations
Avn.	Aviation
BD	Bombardment (later Air) Division
BG	Bombardment (Bomb) Group
BG(H)	Bomb Group (Heavy)
BG(M)	Bomb Group (Medium)
BG(L)	Bomb Group (Light)
Bmr.	Bomber
Bomb	Bombardment
BS	Bombardment (Bomb) Squadron
BW	Bombardment (Bomb) Wing
c.	circa (approximate time period)
Carr.	Carrier
CBI	China-Burma-India (Theater of Operations)
Cmbt.	Combat
Cmd.	Command
Cmdo.	Commando
CO	Commanding Officer
Cmpst.	Composite
Crgo.	Cargo
CW	Combat Wing
DB	Dive Bomber
Det.	Detachment
EAME	European-African-Middle Eastern (Theater of Operations)
ERS	Emergency Rescue Squadron
ETO	European Theater of Operations
F/B	Fighter-Bomber
FG / FtrGrp	Fighter Group
FLAK	Anti-Aircraft Fire
Fld.	Field
Flt.	Flight
Ftr.	Fighter
FS / FtrSqdn	Fighter Squadron
FW / FtrWng	Fighter Wing
GB	Great Britain
GHQ	General Headquarters
GP / Grp.	Group
HQ	Headquarters
Incpt.	Interceptor
LN	Liaison
MTO	Mediterranean Theater of Operations
Mpng.	Mapping
NLS	Night Leaflet Squadron
PS	Photographic Squadron
OBS	Observation
OPS	Operations
QIM	Quick Identification Markings (Allied)
OSS	Office Of Strategic Services (US)
(P) / Prov.	Provisional
PG	Photographic Group
Photo	Photographic
POM	Preparation for Overseas Movement
POW	Prisoner Of War
PR	Photographic Reconnaissance
PRG	Photographic Reconnaissance Group
PS	Photographic Squadron
PTO	Pacific Theater of Operations
Pur.	Pursuit
RAF	Royal Air Force (British)
RCM	Radio Counter Measures
Rcn.	Reconnaissance
RG	Reconnaissance Group
RS	Reconnaissance Squadron
SF	Scouting Force
SHAEF	Supreme Headquarters Allied Expeditionary Force
SOE	Special Operations Executive (British)
Spt.	Support
Sq. / Sqdn.	Squadron
Srch.	Search
Stn.	Station
Tac.	Tactical
Trng.	Training
Tr.	Troop
Trnsp.	Transport
T/O	Theater Of Operations
TRG	Tacitcal Reconnaissance Group
TRS	Tactical Reconnaissance Squadron
Triple-A	Anti-Aircraft Artillery
USA	United States Army
UK	United Kingdom
USN	United States Navy
US	United States
USAAF	United States Army Air Force
USSAFE	United States Strategic Air Forces, Europe
WR	Weather Reconnaissance
Wthr.	Weather
Wng.	Wing

ACKNOWLEDGMENTS

The following individuals and institutions provided invaluable historical data and photo images for the creation of this work;

American Battle Monuments Commission

Eighth Air Force Museum

National Air and Space Museum

P-38 National Association

Planes of Fame/Air Museum

United States Air Force Museum/Wright-Patterson AFB

United States National Archives and Records

8th AF Historical Society

20th Fighter Group Association

31st Fighter Group Association

352nd Fighter Group Association

353rd Fighter Group Association

303rd Bomb Group (H) Association

A special thanks is tendered to the following individuals;

Former USAAF Pilot Lt. (later Cpt.) Robert 'Punchy' Powell

352ndFG, the 'Bluenosed Bastards of Bodney'

93 combat missions, 6 confirmed 'kills'

P-47 Thunderbolts and P-51 Mustangs

'Punchy' supplied me with enough background material on the evolution of Eighth AAF fighter tactics in WWII to fill a book. I hope to share much of this data in future Battle Colors works.

Peter Randell of 'www.littlefriends.co.uk.'

Peters dedication to the preservation of 8th USAAF Fighter history and his willingness to share his knowledge proved to be an invaluable asset in researching material for this work.

Former Sgt./ USAAF Ordinance, Chester Gavryck

Chester's knowledge of aerial ordinance has helped fill in much of the details relating to this subject that are so difficult to locate today. His contribution to the ongoing research for the Battle Colors series will be detailed in upcoming Volume 3.

BIBLIOGRAPHY

Aces And Wingmen/I: Danny Morris
Aircraft Insignia-Spirit Of Youth:
    National Geographic, June 1943/Gerard Hubbard
Air Force Units Of World War II: Dr. M. Maurer
American Eagles/American Volunteers In The RAF/1941-1945:
    Tony Holmes
Battles With The Luftwaffe: Theo Boiten & Martin Bowman
B-25 Mitchell: Bert Kinzey
B-26 Marauder Units of The Eighth And Ninth Air Forces:
    Jerry Scutts
Combat Insignia Stamps Of The United States Army & Navy:
    Hearst Publications
Combat Squadrons Of The Air Force, World War II:
    Dr. M. Maurer
Command And Employment Of Air Power:
    War Department Field Manual/FM 100-20
Fighters Of The Mighty Eighth:
    William N. Hess/Thomas G. Ivie
From The Zenith To The Deck:
    Eighth Fighter Command/Gen. Francis Griswold
Insignia & Decorations Of The US Armed Forces:
    National Geographic, 1944
Jagdwaffe/Holding The West, 1941-1943:
    David Wadman/Martin Pegg
Jagdwaffe/Defending The Reich, 1943-1944:
    Robert Forsyth/Eddie J. Creek
Jagdwaffe/Defending The Reich, 1944-1945: Robert Forsyth
L-Birds/American Combat Liaison Aircraft Of World War II:
    Terry M. Love
Lockheed: Bill Yenne
Martin B-26 Marauder: Fredrick A. Johnsen
Mosquito Photo-Reconnaissance Units Of World War II:
    Martin Bowman
P-38 Lightning:
    Bert Kinzey
Secret Squadrons of the Eighth: Pat Carty
The Army Air Forces In World War II;
    Combat Chronology/ 1941-1945
    Kit C. Carter/Robert Mueller
The Luftwaffe/Strategy For Defeat: Williamson Murray
The Mighty Eighth: Roger Freeman
The Mighty Eighth In Color: Roger Freeman
The Official Guide To The Army Forces:
    Army Air Forces Aid Society
The Organization And Lineage Of The United States Air Force:
    Charles A. Ravenstein
The United States Strategic Bombing Surveys/European War:
    United States Air Force
Tumult In The Clouds: James A. Goodson
USAAF Markings & Camouflage: Robert Archer
War Insignia Stamp Album/Vol's.2,3 & 4:
    Robert Lash Robbins

INDEX

Individuals:

Born of the sun
they traveled a short while towards the sun,
And left the vivid air signed with their honor.
-Steven Bender-